Blessings,

S J Rosen

The

Voice

of the

Spirit

The Voice of the Spirit

First Printing 1999
Updated/Expanded Edition 2010

S.G. ROSE PUBLISHING
www.sgrose.com/thevoiceofthespirit
www.thevoiceofthespirit.com

ISBN 978-0-9842482-0-9

Printed in the United States of America

Cover Photography & Design, S.G.Rose
Calligraphy, S.G.Rose

This book is dedicated to

my Lord and Savior, Jesus Christ

*You have been my guide and my constant companion
throughout my life ~ even before I awoke to Your presence.
You are my example, and Your wisdom has strengthened me,
lifted me, directed me, and saved me.
You are the Way, the Truth, the Life,
and the lover of my soul.
Thank You, dear Jesus, for holding out Your hand
and saying, "Come...follow Me."*

Love and gratitude beyond measure to...

My husband, Lance.

You say you are just a man, but I think you are an angel sent to pour joy
all over my heart. I love you in a million ways, and you have made them
all easy. Words, words, words. I wrote almost all of them before I knew
you. Dreams, dreams, dreams. I opened my eyes and you were real.
Because of you, the vision for this book became reality.
You were always part of God's plan, and are His autumn gift to me.

*I*saac and Jacob, my sons and the stars in my crown.

From the time you arrived it was clear you had come here on quests of
your own. Never despise your battle scars, for they are the marks of
courage and endurance. I thank God for the high calling and privilege of
being your mother on this earth. You have taught my soul.

*A*nd all the cherished family and friends

whose wisdom, support, encouragement, inspiration and love are woven
into the tapestry of my life. Whether we are together or apart, I hold you
forever in the deep places of my heart. May God's face shine upon you,
His touch comfort you, His light guide your steps, and His truth give you
peace. He's waiting at the finish line for all of us.

Contents

Contents

And it shall come to pass
in the last days, says God,
I will pour out of My Spirit on all flesh:
and your sons and your daughters
shall prophesy,
and your young men shall see visions,
and your old men shall dream dreams;
and on My servants and My handmaidens
I will pour out in those days of My Spirit:
and they shall prophesy.

Joel 2:28-29
•
Acts 2:17-18

Dear Reader...

*M*ore than three decades have passed since I began writing this book. Thirty years ago I was young, idealistic, passionate, fearless and eager to test God's promise: *"All things are possible to those who believe."* I owed every good thing in my life to Him, and His light and love filled my days and nights. But it hadn't always been that way.

I attended Sunday school as a child and sang in the church choir as a teenager. The solemn, predictable Sunday morning ritual offered an hour of peaceful refuge that kept me faithful, but I seldom listened to the words of wisdom from the pulpit. Perhaps my subconscious heard, but my mind was usually elsewhere. Home was an emotional battleground, and I was planning escape.

At eighteen, I declared my independence and packed my bags. It was the late Sixties, and we, the notorious baby boomers, had come of age. Intent upon creating our own brave new world, we rejected our parents' old-fashioned ideals and did as we pleased. In less than five years, I'd hit rock bottom.

The events and choices that lead to the brink of self-destruction are different for each person who finds themselves there. What determines which way we turn at the end of that road? When my moment arrived, was it the long-forgotten words of a Sunday school teacher that nudged me in a saving direction? And if so, had those words been part of a master plan? Had my painful passage always been foreseen? Was this culmination the inevitable rebirth my soul had been waiting for?

I contemplate those profound possibilities only in retrospect, for I had no such thoughts that night. I still remember the feelings of loneliness, helplessness and fear that consumed me as I lay curled up in the fetal position weeping like a terrified child. From that black pit of despair, one small, pitiful prayer escaped: *"God, if You are there, please take care of me, because I can't take care of myself anymore."* The words were my soul's last cry. I did not expect an answer.

Part of me believes I am the most blessed person on the planet to have experienced what happened next. A bigger part knows I'm no one special, for God hears the cry of every heart, and responds. Human eyes and ears cannot always perceive His answers, but in the realm of the spirit, events are set in motion.

At the end of my prayer, a painful, ragged sigh escaped my aching chest. The darkness heard it and reached for me. I had no strength to fight off its embrace. My eyelids were raw and swollen from hours of crying and felt like lead. I struggled to hold them open, but finally lost the battle. Surrendering my will, abandoning my life, I let go, and sank into the waiting void.

In the next instant, I found myself in a place filled with brilliant, holy light. There, standing before me, was a man more beautiful than can be imagined. A golden-white aura surrounded him and radiated outward. His eyes met mine and my soul knew Who He was. He stretched out His arms in welcome and I felt drawn toward Him as a child to a beloved parent. The love that poured from Him was beyond anything we experience on earth. It was a force field of vibrant, magnetic energy – all-powerful, all-consuming, all-knowing, and unconditional. I had prayed, God had heard, and He had sent His Son to me.

This was not the Jesus of my childhood story books or the icon depicted in so many solemn paintings. However many of us experience these visions and attempt to describe Him, words will always fail to convey His glory. He is unquestionably the Prince of the Universe, yet wears His sovereignty with great humility. In His presence there is perfect peace, and everything becomes very clear and simple.

My soul had always known Him, but humanity had caused me to forget for a time. He'd been waiting for me, and this was a reunion. I needed to remember Who He was, what He could do, and who I could become because of Him. I believe He wants this for us all.   • *Psalm 139*

In How It Began, which follows, I have written more about this first miraculous encounter with Jesus, how it changed my life, the spiritual forces that became active, and the communications that have followed throughout the years. One of the first was a directive to *"Write the book."* This is that book. I could never have dreamed, when I heard those words while in prayer one day, that I, the young mother, would be a grandmother before it was completed. God has much to teach us and school takes many forms. We cannot testify to the fire until we have felt the flame...to the truth until He reveals the lies...to the miraculous until we see Him demonstrate His power.

In the early years, prophetic words of encouragement from the Father came to me on a number of occasions through other people. They shared a common thread: God was going to give me "many keys." Much further down the road, I came to understand why. The keys weren't just for me, though I desperately needed and used them all. *"I saw a picture in my mind of a prison..."* one person said, *"where a great many innocent, helpless people were locked up in cells. Others visited and spoon-feed them between the bars. After they'd left, you walked in with the keys."*

 I realize that because this book is a compilation of many writings, there's a strong temptation to flip through it and read them at random. While I'm sure God can and will speak to readers that way, I'd like to share the reason why I encourage you to start at the beginning and read straight through.

In 1997, I received God's signal that the time had come for publishing, and plunged whole-heartedly into the task, only to be blocked by the daunting question of how to arrange the seemingly-disconnected writings of thirty-some years. For days, I sorted and shuffled the hundreds of pages dozens of different ways, all of which seemed awkward and disjointed. Finally, it occurred to me that since this book was God's idea, He might have an order in mind. Anxious as I was to move forward, I had learned how to wait on Him (there's a dual meaning to that word *wait*, just as there is to the word *submit*) and I set it all aside, confident that His answer would come.

Months had passed (there's *no* hurrying God) when I awoke one morning with the strong feeling that I was to approach the task again. This time, as though a Divine hand were guiding the process, the pieces fell effortlessly into place within a few minutes. I stared at the perfect flow, wherein each writing built upon the one before it to form a greater message, and said, *"Why couldn't I see that before?"* ...An order not visible from the trenches but clearly seen from the higher perspective of the Holy Spirit, Who had been directing everything from the start.

 I offer the stories, inspirations, visions and prophecies that follow with faith that they will go forth and accomplish what God meant them to. Within these pages, may you find freedom, strength, comfort, confirmation and encouragement, food for your soul and light for your path. I pray you will feel my love and the love of the Father, the Son and the Holy Spirit. You are never alone.

Selah Gayle Rose

⚘

He asked His disciples,
"Who do people say the Son of Man is?"

They replied,
"Some say John the Baptist,
others say Elijah, and still others,
Jeremiah or one of the prophets."

"But what about you?" He asked.
Who do you say I am?"

Simon Peter answered,
"You are the Messiah,
the Son of the Living God."

Jesus replied,
"Blessed are you, Simon Peter,
for this was not revealed to you
by flesh and blood,
but by My Father in Heaven."

⚘

How It Began

In my foregoing message, I shared a vision that changed my life. If I were reading such a testimony, I would be moved, but I would also have a good many questions. God challenges us in Scripture to put even *His* words to the test. He wants us to learn to operate in wisdom and discernment, for our very lives often depend upon it. In the hope of answering some of your questions, I am eager to tell you more about my first miraculous encounter with Christ, the spiritual awakening that followed, and the task I was given to do. It is my enduring conviction that just as the Holy Spirit directed the writing of this book and impressed upon me over so many years that it was to be completed and shared, there is also a reason you hold it in your hands now.

Jesus came to me that night when I cried out for God's help, and the glory of that vision has not dimmed throughout my life. To see Him is to behold God and Man coexisting as one. If I were given but one sentence to describe Him, I would say, *"He is Love, personified."* Divine love literally emanates from His body, surrounds Him and flows outward. I felt irresistibly drawn to step into that holy light and when I did so, profound peace enveloped my being, changing me forever.

To stand in the presence of the King of Kings is to become acutely aware of one's spiritual poverty. My sins were many, and I admitted to them with a broken heart – but the chastisement I expected did not come.

"Forgiven." The word echoed through my soul, and I realized that He had always heard my every thought and felt my every emotion. Then, the knowledge was given to me that He had absorbed all of the pain and sorrow in this world and had overcome them through the power of His love. I saw that He had been with me all my life, waiting for me to ask for His help. My wall of human pride had finally crumbled and now His mercy and compassion flowed to me like a mighty river breaking through a dam. He knew me better than I knew myself, and the incredible relief that came with that assurance was immediately followed by the understanding that He wanted not only to heal me, but to show me how to move beyond the way of life that had trapped me in darkness. Feelings of shame lingered in my heart and I knew He saw them, but He

ignored them and focused instead on my desire to receive what He could give me.

While this supernatural encounter was taking place, my intellect was simultaneously pondering how such a thing could be happening. I knew my physical body was still lying in bed, but that fact was of no interest to the "me" that had been transported into this other heavenly reality with Christ. I wanted and needed everything He was offering, and the moment I chose to move forward into the experience, I found myself no longer standing before Jesus, but resting in His arms. He held me close to His chest as tenderly as if I was a sleeping child. I could feel His heart beating, and for the first time in memory, I felt completely safe.

Then, He directed my attention toward my own inner being, and I saw what He could see there: a stagnant swamp of emotional toxins – pain, fear, anger and more. The sight of this vile repository filled me with revulsion, shame and fear, for it was obviously the cause of my soul sickness, and worse yet, it was the only "well" I had to draw from.

But just as quickly as He had allowed me to see the poisons, Jesus began drawing them out of me. I could actually feel this spiritual "dialysis" happening, and when I realized He was taking them *into His own heart*, profound awe displaced all other thoughts.

The cleansing process was long, and I was sobered by the large volume of contaminated "blood" I'd been holding within. I was enormously thankful that Jesus was taking it away, and felt extreme relief when the last drops left. I knew that I'd been saved from a painful spiritual death and been given the opportunity for a fresh start. I was overwhelmed with gratitude for the mercy, love and grace I'd received – but there was even more to come.

As I rested in Jesus' arms, a transfusion of pure, vibrant, holy energy began to enter and circulate throughout my being. Though I ache to do so, I cannot express the emotions I experienced when I realized that *He was giving me His own precious blood.* Hope and light replaced despair and darkness, and I became a new person. The fear that had filled my mind (could it possibly have been only moments before?!) was gone, and I, though completely undeserving, had been rescued, forgiven, cleansed, healed and given a new life.

Nothing had been required of me but the willingness to walk into my Savior's arms and yield to the process of renewal – but within my heartcry to God, there had been complete surrender to His will. Before we are enlightened, we are convinced that the unbridled exercise of our human will shall bring freedom and satisfaction, when in fact, it results in bondage and sorrow. Before our spirits awaken at our "second birth," we serve ego, and view submission to God as constraining and oppressive, when in fact, it is the *only* path to true freedom, power, and unending joy.

I did not ever want those euphoric moments of healing and transformation in Jesus' arms to end! I wonder if we feel that way in our mother's womb – blissfully submitted to, dependent upon and nourished only by love. I don't think I recognized the experience as my second birth while it was happening, but I realized later that it was. And I could never turn back again.

From that moment forward, I wanted only to know the Son of God better and to live in the circle of that amazing love. But I was still on the planet, and if I'd thought trouble would never touch my life again, I had only to look at my Savior's life to know better. My journey had just begun.

૭

3

his
is what the Lord,
the God of Israel says:
"Write in a book
all the words I have spoken
to you."

❧ Jeremiah 30:2 ❧

"Write the Book"

From that first night when God's Son came to me until now, nothing is sweeter than the certain expectation that when I talk to my Father, He will answer me. Sometimes He speaks first and I just listen. No amount of skepticism or ridicule (and I've endured both) can diminish the reality of the Father, Son and Holy Spirit, for Their living presence is with me always.

In the years that followed my spiritual awakening, I married and gave birth to two sons, a business, and countless hopes and aspirations. Each day's to-do list demanded every ounce of my energy, and quiet stolen moments alone with God were precious and restorative. The children's afternoon nap time was the perfect opportunity, and I spent it in prayer as often as I could. On one such day, I'd barely closed my eyes when my attention was commanded by a vivid image that seemed to have been projected into my mind. It was the cover of a book. Mystified, I asked God why He was showing it to me.

"You will write this book," came the answer. *I would?* How? I wasn't a writer. What was it about? I re-read the title and saw a description of the contents below it. I pressed, *"What do You mean, **I'm** going to write it?"* This time my question went unanswered.

Days and weeks passed. The picture and God's words remained stuck firmly in the front of my mind while I tried to figure out how to carry out the commission. As I'd seen that the book was a collection of writings, my first strategy was to make appointments with pastors, priests and other respected spiritual leaders, whom I anticipated would provide plenty of inspiring material. We met in church offices, at coffee shops, and over lunch, but when told of God's directive and how honored I'd be if they would be willing to share something for inclusion in the book, their reactions were always the same: *"Hmmm...well, I'm flattered that you'd ask, but I can't really think of anything specific."*

In light of how well-known and respected these folks were, it was hard to believe that they had nothing to contribute. Perhaps they felt it would be too risky to associate their good names with a woman who believed she'd received a mandate from The Almighty, but whatever the reason, their lack of enthusiasm was disheartening.

I was ready and willing to do whatever God asked, but no more flashes of insight came. Many months went by, and I learned to live with the picture branded on the inside of my forehead. It never left, but I finally stopped asking questions. Every now and then I wondered if I'd completely misunderstood the message. I didn't admit defeat, but I had no clue how to accomplish the directive.

Almost a year had passed, when during another afternoon prayer time, Jesus came to me in a vision. I recorded that experience and titled it *The Path*. New spiritual vistas were revealed, a floodgate opened, and from that day forward, the contents of the book God said I would write poured into my heart and onto the page.

Some messages came in whispers and others as lightning bolts, but they all came at unexpected moments. I was often awakened in the middle of the night to write as the Holy Spirit spoke. If an inspiration came while I was driving, I'd pull over and write it down, for God's words were so far above my own natural thoughts that I feared I wouldn't be able to reconstruct what He'd said later from memory. Some prophecies were dictated word for word. On other occasions I'd hear only the first sentence, but when I was obedient to record it, a larger truth would emerge and unfold. I learned to keep pen and paper close at hand and will forever treasure my tattered old collection of grocery store receipts, restaurant napkins and other scraps of paper upon which I scribbled God's precious words.

I cannot explain how this all happened, or why God chose me for the task. When Jesus saved my life I gave it back to Him and asked to be of service. I'm pretty certain He welcomes such offers.

God's messages overflowed the confines of this book long ago, but the Holy Spirit has always been specific about the contents, and the writings that aren't included have gone out in other ways. Some were penned under my former name and distributed through the inspirational gift line I produced for many years. They've since been re-printed by others and circulated worldwide. And of course, God willing, there will be more messages, stories and books to come. I love my job and my assignment never changes: to listen with an open heart, and to share the Holy Spirit's words when prompted.

The road has not been an easy one, and it has seemed, at times, that the steep and narrow way has held more than one person's fair share of trials, slippery slopes and sorrows. I did not know, in the beginning, what lay before me, although Jesus tried to prepare me for it during the vision of *The Path* and the message of *The Rose*. But, as He promised, He has been beside me through every dark hour. When I feel lost, helpless, confused or afraid, I reach for His hand, seek His wisdom and listen for His voice. Never for an instant can I imagine life without Him. It would just be way too hard.

My faith is experiential. It is in the person of Jesus Christ, not in anything conceived, organized, built or operated by humans. It is not in religion or the religious, not in governments, laws, dogma, doctrines, philosophies, institutions, clubs, committees, gurus, teachers, preachers or leaders of this world. They are all fallible.

In the early years of my zeal to serve God I allowed myself to be convinced that credentials were important, and became a licensed, ordained minister. People care; God doesn't. He hands out crowns, not diplomas. He does not divide up or categorize His children – He endows them with gifts and gives their lives purpose. Many people are religious about what they believe and the causes they support and promote. That does not make them Godly. The Pharisees of Jesus' day were religious. He called them *"...whitewashed tombs full of dead men's bones and every other unclean thing."* • Matthew 23:27

Should someone label me "religious" because I am a follower of Christ and a seeker of truth, I will be quick to correct them. I want only to be what Jesus said we are: *salt.* We were never intended to sit around stuck together in containers getting lumpy. We're meant to be poured out as seasoning for this world. That's a relief to me, for those who know me best will tell you I'm far more salty than sweet.

"You are the salt of the earth. But if the salt loses its saltiness,
how can it be made salty again?   It is no longer good for anything..."
• Matthew 5:13

The truths God's Spirit has asked me to share have proven themselves repeatedly in the nitty-gritty stuff of life. They're as old as the universe and its Creator, Who consistently reveals Himself in new ways to new generations. They are eternal principles that operate regardless of whether humans believe or not. Throughout the ages, there have always been *"those with an ear to hear what the Spirit is saying."* Countless numbers have heard and have shared the messages they were given. I'm just one little alto voice in a massive choir.   • Revelations 3:2

In the beginning especially, every communication I received sent me on an enthusiastic search for validation. Without fail, I would discover it in one or more places within the Bible. I still apply this test, and no matter how many times the confirmations are revealed, I am always awed. I've concluded that the Biblical passages are there to be found because their truths, like their Divine Author, never change.

I did not study the Bible first and paraphrase its teachings for the writings in this book. It was the opposite. When I first began to receive the visions and messages, I knew little of the scriptures, but as each quest for corroboration led me deeper, I discovered the meaning of *"The Living Word."* What God was saying to me, He'd been saying to others throughout time. References to many of those companion Biblical texts are included throughout this book, and I guarantee that you will be greatly enriched when you read them.

Though He loves me, God has not spared me all pain. You will read my tears on the pages of this book, but you'll hear my laughter, too. One purges, the other heals – and each have their season. I've also learned to abandon any desire to dictate what might enter my life, and when. Expectations disappoint more often than not, a closed mind doesn't leave God room for surprises, and many of the things I used to think were important, really aren't.

I've made some spectacular trips to the mountain top, but most of my time has been spent trudging through the valley in worn out sneakers. I've loved, trusted unreservedly, and felt Judas' kiss. I've watched helplessly while plans and dreams that seemed to have God's stamp of approval all over them have disintegrated in mid-flight. I've started over...and over...and over, each time becoming more aware of my human vulnerabilities and the sovereignty of my God.

This book is about the painful, glorious process of enlightenment, the truths that are exposed and the lessons we learn when we are willing to submit to the process of being changed into the image of the One Who gave us life. He is preparing us for the life after this one.

"He is the Potter, we are the clay." • Isaiah 64:8

God's fingerprints are all over my life, and I want it no other way. He knows what He's doing, and if you've ever watched a potter slap down a lopsided pot and start over from scratch, you will understand the prophet Isaiah's metaphor.

I remember sobbing, once, over some now long-forgotten drama, petitioning God for His sympathy and support. *"Oh Lord, they have hurt me so! They don't understand me, but **You** know my heart..."*

8

I wanted to hear, *"There, there Sweetheart...tell me who they are and I'll take care of them."* But instead, a strong correction came:

*"Why do you keep telling me what's in your heart as though I don't already know? My child, I know the depths of your heart better than you **ever** will!"*

I'm still humbled by the enormity of that statement, and since I never forget that I am *always* known better than I know myself, I've stopped trying to get away with much. I no longer ask *"Why me?"* because I know the answer. No difficulty is allowed without our Father's knowledge. The fruit of suffering is compassion. It's all chaos with purpose and He sustains and guides His people. Everything – *absolutely everything* – is going according to Divine plan.

A messenger does not seek to build his or her own kingdom. Time may pass while we hold the words in our hearts. We must test them first, for we do not take our commissions lightly. God is not offended by our questions, and inquiry does not diminish, alter or destroy truth – it reveals and validates it.

When a message is meant to be shared, an urging will persist – the inescapable feeling that we have not yet completed the work we were asked to do. We can push this feeling aside and fill our lives with everything else that demands our time and attention, but it does not leave. It grows stronger when we read or hear a portion of the same message through another person. We feel an instant kinship with these souls even if we have never met them. And messengers can drag their feet at times too. It takes courage to speak, for we know others will judge us.

Those who wish to find their purpose and complete their task on this earth discover that these things cannot be accomplished by their own power or strength of will. Spiritual commissions succeed through the surrender of self in quiet, humble obedience. There's no room for personal agendas, however righteous they may be. God ignores them. Unlike human goals and desires, those of eternal significance are fulfilled not by our own might but by God's decision.

In this job, you learn to allow time to pass when you know you're running out; to wait on the shore when you would rather launch; and to let go of what you hold dear to follow God into the unknown.

"How can I be like you?" a much younger me fervently asked a servant of God who was more Christ-like than anyone I've ever met.

"Oh, that's easy," he smiled gently. *"You have to die."*

☙

S. G. Rose

Visions & Dreams

Imagination is a powerful gift bestowed upon us by our Creator. God drops inspirations into our consciousness like seeds and encourages us to work *with* Him, that they might manifest on earth *("...Thy Kingdom come, Thy will be done, on earth as it is in Heaven.")* Many inventors and artists attest to receiving ideas in dreams or visions. The ability to imagine, visualize, and create is an attribute of our Father's nature within *all* of us, for we are His children, created in His image. Though we do not all exercise the creative powers of our heritage, we *all* possess them.

Dreams can be insightful, encouraging, inspiring, revealing, reassuring or even prophetic. Our Father speaks to us in any way He chooses, and since we all dream, I suspect that millions of people hear from Him quite regularly without realizing it.

Most of our answers lie within, but the unrelenting analysis of the conscious mind can muddy the waters, making it difficult for us to see them. During sleep, the subconscious mind sorts and processes the information and emotions that have been registered (and/or suppressed) by the waking mind. The data is then re-framed and played back for our review in pictorial form, giving us the opportunity to more objectively acknowledge, approach and resolve the issues presented. We *need* to dream.

Opportunities can be missed when dreams are ignored. The fact that some dreams linger – or even recur – as though entreating us to decipher their symbols, probably means we're supposed to be doing that. Even though our culture does not commonly promote it, the rewards we receive from taking the time to interpret our dreams are well worth the effort. An understanding of how to approach dream interpretation, plus help from the Holy Spirit, can result in some amazing insights.

Prophetic, directive and revelatory dreams are in a category of their own. The Bible cites many examples of God communicating through prophetic dreams, and my own personal experience has convinced me of their occurrence and validity. I've been visited, comforted, guided, informed, warned, and shown things I had no possible way of knowing. Such dreams have been irrefutable evidence of my Heavenly Father's watchful care and guidance. Sometimes they've delivered revelations that were critical to a life-path choice – and at other times, they've prepared me for what lay ahead.

If a dream is revelatory or prophetic, yet does not relate to an immediate situation, it will remain in one's mind – possibly for years – until its directive has been understood or its purpose achieved. Until that time, confirmations will continue to present themselves during the course of the dreamer's everyday life – reminders so obvious and specific that they cannot be dismissed as coincidence. These signs seem to be sent to reinforce the importance of the dream so that it will not be forgotten.

Some of the prophetic dreams I've received over the years still await fulfillment, yet they remain as clear in memory as when I awoke from them. I have not stopped contemplating their possible symbolism, and I rest assured that the day will come, as it always has in the past, when I will see the events they foretold come to pass before my eyes.

A vision is a supernatural experience initiated by a force greater than ourselves to impart an understanding higher than our own conscious thoughts. We sense a Divine presence, seen or unseen, are known by this companion, and feel completely safe, loved and accepted. Our emotional response is profound and we are held in wonder. Our minds and souls acknowledge, accept and embrace what is revealed.

Visions are tangible to the soul, and those who have had them must attempt to describe the indescribable. Such an experience is unique to the mind of its beholder, so my above definition may be broad by some standards or too confining by others.

From the brief appearance of an unexpected image or message within the mind, to the sense of leaving the physical body and being taken to another location, visions have been reported and recorded throughout the ages.

During these encounters with the Divine, we are mentally awake and alert. We become aware of a spiritual body which we find to be familiar, comfortable and superior to our earthly one, causing us to experience detachment from (and/or disinterest in) our fleshly body. All our senses are heightened; we feel calm and energized, and our minds are sharp.

Visions that share the characteristics of "near-death" or "life-after-death" experiences can have the same dramatic, life-changing effect. In them, we hear and understand our Guide without words being spoken out loud. We're free to ask questions, and may even be invited to do so, while what we are intended to see and learn is being revealed. Though profound feelings of reverence, humility and awe overwhelm us, these are soothed with understanding, patience and gentleness. A pure, harmonious flow of light and energy connects all matter, colors are vibrant far beyond their subdued earthly versions, and each individual creation is an exquisite masterpiece of design and form. Our enhanced senses take it all in, and even the smallest details – whether near or on a distant horizon – are easily visible to the eye. Those whose visions take them to Heavenly realms report feeling as though they have returned to the place their soul calls Home.

"...For now we see through a glass darkly,
but then, face to face...
Now I know in part,
but then, I shall know, even as I am known."
*
St. Paul
I Corinthians13:11

And it shall come to pass
in the last days, says God,
I will pour out of My Spirit on all flesh:
and your sons and your daughters
shall prophesy,
and your young men shall see visions,
and your old men shall dream dreams...'
*
Acts 2:17-18

S.G.Rose

14

The Path

Talking often with the Father in prayer deepens and strengthens our relationship with Him. Asking Him to inspire and direct our prayers paves the way for miracles.

To submit one's heart and mind to Spirit-led prayer is to become a receiver and transmitter of power. First, we ask to be attuned to His voice, and after that, we simply make ourselves available and wait. When He speaks, we listen with a yielded heart and respond as He leads. If we do these things, we will find that our own desires intertwine with those of our Father.

Praying according to the will of God is surprisingly simple. When we become as children who run to His arms when He calls, He will embrace us and draw us to His heart. No urging from the Spirit is without purpose or reason whether revealed to us or not. If God brings someone to mind, and we respond by praying for them, we can be assured that angels have been dispatched and forces set in motion.

How incredible it is to know that the doorway to this communion *always* stands open...and that when we enter, He will share the mysteries of His kingdom with us!

One quiet summer afternoon my heart was suddenly stirred by a deep longing to be alone with Jesus, to walk with Him and to share His companionship. I stopped what I was doing, knelt down in my warm, sunlit bedroom, and expressed this to Him in prayer. I didn't know that this desire had been placed in my heart by the Holy Spirit and that Jesus was already waiting for me.

I closed my eyes, and in the next heartbeat I found myself standing near an unfamiliar trailhead at twilight. I knew, of course, that it was my spirit, not my physical body which had been transported there, but just as had happened in the vision years before when Christ had first appeared to me, I was so drawn into the experience that my spiritual form felt more real than the body I had "left behind." The first thing I noticed was that my senses had all become remarkably acute. Every sight, smell and sensation was amplified far beyond what we experience in the flesh.

The air was damp and the smells of earth and stone were pungent. As I looked around, I realized my eyesight was extraordinarily sharp and clear, and that the glasses I wore to correct severe nearsightedness were gone. I could feel each individual particle of moisture within the cool gray mist as it settled on the skin of my arms, and I shivered as I tried to adjust to the dramatic change in temperature. I looked down at my bare feet, and even while a part of me argued that the concern was ridiculous, since I was not actually there in the flesh, I thought, *"I'm not dressed for this place...I'm not even wearing shoes!"*

An immense dark mountain filled my field of vision, and standing before me at its base was Jesus. He was wearing a white, linen robe, and I noticed that He, too, was barefoot. He held out His hand, and although He did not speak out loud, my heart heard His invitation, *"Would you like to come with me? I have something to show you."*

I eagerly accepted, and immediately when I took His hand, He turned and led me toward a narrow pathway which had appeared in the darkness behind Him. He set out at a brisk pace and I hurried to keep up. I marveled that I could feel the hard ground beneath my feet and the dust between my toes, because my active reasoning was still operating on a parallel track, reminding me that this was a vision, not a physical reality. (That internal debate ceased a short time later when the experience demanded all my focus.)

After a short distance, the path suddenly grew narrower and steeper, and the vegetation disappeared. An ominous-looking wall of slick black slate jutted upward on our right and disappeared into the darkness above. Razor-sharp shards of stone littered the ground. As we climbed, the wall bit deeper into the path, narrowing it until our shoulders were brushing against the unyielding rock face. To our left the ground dropped off abruptly, and when I ventured a glance over the edge, I found myself looking down into the impenetrable blackness of a bottomless abyss. Strangely, although we were walking along its very edge, I felt no fear of falling into it. I did instinctively tighten my grasp on Jesus' hand, however, and in response, He told me that I need not – and should not – look down into it again.

By that point, it had become obvious that this stroll with my Lord was not going to be what I'd had in mind when I'd first prayed. I wasn't much of a hiker, and the trail that had appeared fairly easy at the beginning was now testing my endurance. Those facts were overridden by my desire to see what He wanted to show me, but I started to wonder if I was strong enough to make it the rest of the way. He heard the questions within my mind and answered them.

"I'll never let go of you. As long as you hold My hand, you'll be safe."

Jesus climbed effortlessly. It was obvious that He had covered the ground countless times while guiding others like myself up the mountain. He knew exactly where each solid foothold was to be found and it became imperative that I step in precisely the same spots to keep from slipping or stumbling. I was astounded that I was able to climb so well and that the jagged rocks were not bruising or cutting the soles of my feet as it seemed they should have been. As I contemplated this, I realized that I was being supernaturally enabled to follow Him.

Whether these understandings, or the fact that we had not rested during the long climb made me vulnerable, I do not know, but suddenly a wave of extreme weariness engulfed me, and with it came a flood of anxious, fearful doubts. What if Jesus' confidence in me was misplaced? My common sense argued that even if He held my hand, this trail was too hard for me. How high *was* this mountain, anyway? What made Him think I could do this? What if I had to give up? How would I find my way back? What if I lost my balance and fell into the abyss?

Whereas I had been filled with courage and confidence moments before, as soon as I allowed myself to entertain these negative thoughts, a terrible stab of fear twisted my stomach into a knot and threatened to paralyze me. I fought it, hoped Jesus hadn't sensed my panic, and gripped His hand tighter. My legs felt like lead, but I kept moving. The sight of His back in front of me was my only comfort. He continued to climb and I watched every step He took. I could, and *would* climb, too. But if I hadn't fully understood before, I knew now that if I let go of His hand or took my eyes off of Him for even an instant, I would be lost.

Jesus looked back over His shoulder at me and His expression conveyed He'd heard my thoughts and knew that I comprehended the serious nature of our journey. Again, without spoken words, He explained that the crippling thoughts were lying voices from the abyss and that I must learn to ignore them. He reassured my heart and admonished me not to fear, for my safe arrival at our destination was His responsibility, and He would not fail me. I felt renewed, refreshed, and my anticipation grew. Where were we going? What awaited us there? He heard my eager questions but did not answer.

There was no sense of time in that place, so I cannot say how long we climbed. The trail dwindled to a foot-wide ledge in the black wall, and up ahead it disappeared altogether. The summit was finally in view above, but it seemed impossible to get to, especially in such darkness.

Jesus paused, looked upward, and the sky began to fill with light similar to the aurora borealis but far more beautiful. Holiness vibrated within it and the sight of it filled my soul with joy. I reasoned that such glory could only be emanating from Heaven – so, *that* must be our destination! Delighted with myself for guessing His surprise, I thanked Jesus profusely, told Him that I now understood why it had been worth the perilous climb, and that I could hardly wait to get there. He made no reply to my exuberant chatter, but I was too excited to wonder about His silence.

In the next instant – I cannot explain how, for I have no memory of it – we were on top of the mountain. My legs were weak with excitement and I rested for a moment while I got my bearings. Ours was the highest peak within a massive mountain range that encircled a magnificent valley. Jesus was standing at the edge of the small, flat summit with his back to me, and I went to His side. He was gazing out over the vast expanse below and appeared lost in thought. The vista seemed to spread out to the four points of the compass – as though the entire surface of the earth had been visually compacted and laid out flat before us. The sight was overwhelming and I could not take it all in.

Although comprised of familiar elements, the scene was surreal. The four seasons enveloped various regions within the valley so that some were covered by winter snow; others were alive with new life; others basked in the sun; and still others were aflame with autumn color. Portions of the terrain glowed with soft light, others shimmered gold, and others were dark and foreboding. Shadows and mists drifted across the landscape, silvery rivers and streams coursed through canyons and wound through pastures on their way to seas. Forests, deserts, gardens, jungles, plains, swamplands, oceans and islands – all lay there within the valley.

When I tried to grasp how this could possibly be, Jesus gave me the understanding that I was looking not only upon all of Nature, but also upon the landscape of *time* on this planet. All of the ages – past, present and to come – were represented there. My human mind could not comprehend this. It was too much, too big, too far beyond my ability. I did not understand why Jesus had brought me to see it or what He wanted me to know.

In response, He turned His attention fully to me, put His arm around my shoulders and watched my face as He revealed the reason for our journey. I knew He could read every thought written in my heart, and that He was waiting for my reaction. He drew my eyes to a focal point central to the entire majestic scene below, and I saw with piercing clarity, the source of the holy light. It was not radiating from Heaven as I had assumed. It was streaming from a barren mound where three crude crosses stood.

The emotional force of this revelation was almost more than I could bear, for within that same instant, the filter of human reason was removed, and my spirit was allowed to *experience* the agony and excruciating glory of what had taken place on that day, along with its full impact on everything in existence before and after it. I knew that unrestrained, the emotions would literally have crushed my heart, but Jesus kept that from happening.

Though I had accepted His sacrifice for my own personal redemption, I had never understood it to be *the pivotal event in the history of planet Earth.* Now, I saw that all life is dependent upon Him. Before, I'd viewed His creation and crucifixion through human eyes, but He'd brought me to the mountain top to see it through *His* eyes.

I turned to look at the One whose supreme act of love was and is still belittled, dismissed, despised and rejected by so many for whom He gave Himself. He stood beside me, quietly looking down at the hill where He surrendered His human life, and I saw no sorrow – only acceptance, and almighty, omnipotent power.

Long, silent moments passed on the mountain top while I struggled to absorb and grasp what I was being shown. My Savior knew a human mind could not. Nodding toward the valley, He asked me a question, and watched my face for the answer.

"Are you willing to go there with Me?"

Was I ready to travel with Him through the valley, across the deserts, rivers and oceans below? Would I follow Him through the shadows to the place of His cross and then beyond – just as I had followed Him up this mountain? Were my love and my desire to be with Him that strong? I looked into those eyes of love and answered without hesitation. He had known from the moment I took His hand at the base of the mountain what my reply would be.

"Yes, Lord! I will follow You anywhere."

His smile ignited a fire in my heart. I could feel His anticipation as He assured me that although the adventure ahead was going to be difficult at times, He would sustain and protect me, just as He'd done thus far. Then, He lifted His hand and pointed to the horizon beyond the furthest mountains and I saw our destination. We were going home.

S.G.Rose

20

The Cross

We've scattered its image everywhere
carved and painted, etched in stone and flesh
cast in gold, silver, brass and tin
adorning our bodies
attesting to faith
or thoughtless fashion trend.

Proudly on display

it speaks a thousand words
or none
in the churches, the graveyards
and the dollar store.

Do we think

our symbols and charms hold the power
to save us from ourselves?
Or do we think at all?

Was it the Savior's hope

to be remembered bleeding and broken –
to hang throughout the ages?

Or was the plan

for us to comprehend the love that led Him there?

Forgive us, Lord

We know not what we do.

♦

S.G.Rose

The Adventure

"...An exciting and dangerous undertaking..." Webster

To experience the adventure that awaits in the realm of the spirit, those who have begun the journey know that the first steps, and all those that follow, must be taken by faith. There is no other way to go there. Our infinite souls were created to explore unseen dimensions just as our finite bodies carry within them the yearning to explore this earth. We are more than flesh and blood, and more exists within and around us than can be seen with human eyes. To search out these other domains is our birthright. What we find there will enlighten and transform us, and with this higher knowledge we will better understand our purpose here.

Jesus said, *"The Kingdom of God is within you."* • Luke 17:21 Yet many of us were never shown how to go within, nor were we told it is just as important, if not more so, to explore this sacred inner terrain as it is to find our place in the physical world. Furthermore, if we talk about these matters much, we risk being called dreamers, religious fanatics or fools.

Human beings are body, mind and spirit, yet the notion exists that while we must nurture the body and mind, our souls can be left empty, untended, untrained, unfed and ignored. The result is a gnawing sense that something is missing. Those who do not recognize (or care to know) what that "something" is, will spend their lives unwittingly trying to fill the emptiness in carnal ways – only to fail.

Like the earth changes which re-shape our world and our lives, spiritual awakenings also come. Change is a certainty, for it is the nature of the universe in which we live, and within it are new beginnings.

We humans, however, are creatures of habit. We like our comfort zones, and *don't* like it when our lives and plans are interrupted or our beliefs challenged. Only when we are brave enough to open our eyes and hearts, will we see how much more we yet have to learn. To embrace positive change is to grow, and to it embrace it often is to grow much.

History inspires us with stories of heroes and heroines whose passions for truth and righteousness changed the world and led millions into freedom and enlightenment. It also saddens and sobers us with the tragic accounts of scores of souls who were deceived by the leaders and/or belief systems they chose to follow. How many of these, I wonder, did not understand that the guidance they sought had always been available to each of them directly from its Source? As a recipient of God's unconditional, amazing grace while I was still lost in darkness, my heart believes that in the end, when such souls are set free, the same omnipotent love that reached for me shows them the way home.

Many empowering, liberating revelations have been imparted to mankind by our Creator, yet there are always those who seem determined to grind up these organic truths, refine them, and add their own artificial ingredients in a campaign to target, control and enslave religious shoppers. When a spiritual seeker buys into one of these packages, the supplemental laws, dogma and rituals bring bondage, not freedom. Within these systems, truth is subtly twisted and/or meted out only in part. The creed requires that everyone believe the same, and independent thought is vigorously discouraged or forbidden, encouraging unhealthy dependencies on the leaders. In such environments, the growth of greater understanding that God intended to come from His first precious seeds is stunted, starved and often stamped out altogether.

Adult babies line up by the millions waiting to be fed and entertained, so this marketing obviously works. They consume whatever is served up, and as long as it's popular or convenient, they do not question its purity. In the same way that a diet of fast food threatens physical health, the spiritual well-being and strength of these masses is in serious question. Because their faith is misplaced, when their guru or figurehead falls off of his/her pedestal (as they often ultimately do), the followers are thrown into confusion and turmoil. Trust and faith suffer collateral damage, and some of the wounded even turn completely away from God – Who was the only One who ever had the power to deliver them in the first place. I've lost count of how many such disillusioned victims I have met. Some cloak their pain and confusion with anger, and there's no convincing them that Jesus had nothing to do with the betrayal they've suffered. So, they "throw the baby out with the bathwater."

We are all without excuse. The truth is free to everyone and is always waiting for us outside of the boxes. Our Creator desires a *personal* relationship with *each and every one of us* and He is no respecter of persons, political parties or religious affiliations.

"For since the creation of the world God's invisible qualities –
His eternal power and Divine nature – have been clearly seen, being

understood from what has been made, so that people are without excuse." • Romans 1:20

*O*nce awakened spiritually, we become like a highly sensitive satellite dish focused on the heavens. Our challenge is then to discern which signals – amongst all those we are capable of receiving – are of genuine value and worthy of our focus, otherwise the result will be confusion, crossed signals and a lot of meaningless noise.

The soul of a seeker cries out for only one thing: *Truth.* Truth is more important than any pain we may have to go through to find it. We should not desire to be spoon-fed by others or allow ourselves to become overwhelmed and confused by all of the different items on the spiritual menu of this age. If we want pure truth we must tap into the Source ourselves. Nature can teach us this process and Our Creator intended it to, long before anyone ever preached a sermon or wrote a book.

*I*n Jesus' story of *The Sower,* He compares the *"words of the Kingdom"* to seeds which fall upon many different types of ground.

> *"Once there was a man who went out to sow grain. As he scattered the seed in the field, some of it fell along the path, and the birds came and ate it up. Some of it fell on rocky ground, where there was little soil. The seeds soon sprouted because the soil wasn't deep. But when the sun came up it burned the young plants; and because the roots had not grown deep enough the plants soon dried up. Some of the seed fell among thorn bushes which grew up and choked the plants. But some seeds fell in good soil and the plants bore grain: some had one hundred grains, others sixty, and others thirty...*
>
> *"Listen, then, and learn what the parable of the sower means. Those who hear the message about the Kingdom but do not understand it are like the seeds that fell along the path. The evil one comes and snatches away what was sown in them. The seeds that fell on rocky ground stand for those who receive the message gladly as soon as they hear it. But it does not sink deep into them and they don't last long. So when trouble or persecution comes because of the message, they give up at once. The seeds that fell among thorn bushes stand for those who hear the message; but the worries about this life and the love for riches choke the message, and they don't bear fruit.*

*And the seeds sown in the good soil stand for those who hear
the message and understand it: they bear fruit, some as much
as one hundred, others sixty, and others thirty."*

Matthew 13:3-8, 18-23

If our desire is to be *"good soil"* in which truth can flourish, the
process must begin with tilling up the hardened ground and working in
the fertilizer that has been dumped on our lives until our hearts are soft
and ready for planting.

A friend, who is a much-loved inspirational speaker, once told
me that people often ask her what they need to do in order to be like her.

"They want the fruit," she lamented, *"but they never want to
hear about the manure!"*

everyone hopes to avoid difficulties, hardships and heartaches,
and it's no surprise that they are often referred to as manure by different
names. They are, however, inevitable, and there's little growth without
them. I'm not saying we should expect to drown in dung, for that's
unhealthy in the opposite extreme, but at the times when its piled at our
feet, we're being presented with the opportunity to learn how to process it
appropriately and use it to our advantage.

There have been stretches in my life when it seemed like my
house was a regular stop on the manure truck's route. It came so often
that my ears became attuned to the dreaded sound of its engine in the
distance. Desperately I'd pray, *"Oh, dear God, please let it be headed
somewhere else!"* Then, I'd peek out from behind the curtains, only to
witness, with sinking heart, the flashing tail lights and warning beeps as it
backed down the driveway to dump its smelly payload. Finally, one day
when the mountain of problems had already reached the absurd, I heard it
coming down the road *again*, and something snapped. Instead of
dreading its arrival, I laughed and shouted, *"Thank You, Lord! You must
really love me to keep sending all this fertilizer!"* He laughed with me
and I've never viewed those deliveries the same way again. They are,
believe it or not, gifts of growth.

When He sees that our heart is soft and ready, we will feel God
plant His seeds of knowledge and truth. When the seedlings first emerge,
we must guard and protect them, for opposing forces will be looking for
an opportunity to trample and uproot the new life.

As the attributes of our Father's nature grow within us, we will need to diligently weed out anything which threatens to choke them. The weeds (cares) of this world will always press in to try to reclaim the ground of our minds and hearts. Dry spells, too, will come, and deep watering with the promises of God's Word will be critical to survival.

Finally, when the harvest is ripe, let us remember to offer the increase back to God, for all good things come from Him to begin with. We honor Him when we share with others what He grew within us. *"Freely you have received...freely give."*

*L*ike our bodies and minds, our spirits require certain nutrients to thrive. When they are hungry, children cry for food. You cannot convince them that it's optional. You cannot stop them from thinking, questioning, imagining, experimenting or creating, either. These are natural, essential processes of growth.

Doesn't it follow that a human soul will seek nourishment and expression as well? Deprived, it will shrivel and ache, but unlike the physical body in which it is housed, it will never die. The body takes in food; the mind, knowledge; the spirit and soul, truth. We know we must be careful of the food we eat. Shouldn't we likewise be cautious about what we feed our minds and souls? Like impure or inadequate food, some of the information presented to us can be polluted, dangerous or even deadly.

What happens when we realize that we have been misled? When we have consumed and been infected by a lie? We become afraid to trust again. But fear is the enemy of truth and the opposite of faith. If we have fallen into deception we feel foolish and victimized. If those feelings simmer for very long, we risk becoming bitter, cynical, critical and hardhearted – all of which are just ugly masks that hide underlying pain and insecurity. Few of us will leave this planet never having been deceived, lied to or betrayed. This is an imperfect world full of imperfect people, all in the process of enlightenment.

*W*e are given a Divine promise, an assurance that if we do not give up we *will* find Truth.

"Ask, and you shall receive. Seek, and you shall find. Knock, and the door shall be opened to you." • Jesus' words in Matthew 7:7

The words denote action. An active spiritual search is an adventure that will never go unrewarded, even though there may be a few

27

rough detours and stumbling blocks along the way. It can take us a lifetime to open our eyes but it takes only an instant to see. The gift of our Creator is free will. The choice to continue to seek is ours.

I have never met a single person who was not acquainted with heartbreak, struggle or suffering. No matter how much we've been through there is a positive side to it all: It will change us. *How* it changes us is our decision. Will it make us bitter, or sweet? Tender or hard? Compassionate or critical? Defensive or discerning? When we defend our own stubbornness or judge someone else who is making a noble effort to change, we are selling short the power of the Spirit.

*"With God, **all** (not 'some') things are possible!"* • Matthew 19:26

We *can* change our thinking (which will change our actions), our habits (which will change our thinking), our actions and reactions (which will change our emotions), our outlook (which will change our future), our attitudes (which will change our outlook), our hearts (which will change our purpose) and thereby, our lives – but it takes courage.

Those who seek will discover.
Those who discover will learn.
Those who learn will be transformed day by day.
The greatest adventure is

*G*rowth.

಄

Words

The power of one
Can build or destroy
A world.

Yes.

No.

Speak into existence
Or turn to dust.

The warmth of *"Hello"*
The emptiness of *"Good-bye."*

When I saw your face
Your eyes smiled
Unlocked my secret heart
Your words reached for me
Mine met you halfway
We began.

Silence is not golden
Until it knows you.
It's darkness
A void
Stillness without form
Leaving all to the imagination.

Talk to me always
In the light.

Create with me.

≈

S.G.Rose

Ordinary People

Human nature never changes. In this present age, we should be grateful, I suppose, that we have a smorgasbord of resources to help us understand our own psyches. Our eyes can be opened to who we are and why we do what we do. The tools to liberate ourselves from our repeat-behavior traps are available to one and all, and the how-to steps of positive change are ours for the asking.

I appreciate many of the books that have been written in this regard, and some of them have helped me enormously. However, there are now more of them out there than I can possibly find time to read. The road to self-improvement is long, and since so many authors have addressed so many different human failings, I now calculate that I would need to read one book right after another until the day I depart the planet in order to cover all of the ground that my nagging imperfections say I should. The problem is, although I know I should always be working on myself, sometimes I just want to relax and be me – flaws and all. I know I'm not the only one who feels this way, but guilt is a powerful motivator and the ever-expanding bookstore section devoted to *Psychology and Self Help* is testimony that people are still looking for answers and can never get enough.

One book outsells them all, but apparently many people buy it the same way I grab the occasional diet and exercise book – with a fanfare of good intentions that inevitably degenerate over time into the deluded belief that the book will magically do its job because I spent money on it and gave it a place of honor on the coffee table.

The all-time best seller I'm referring to is the greatest collection of manuscripts on human psychology ever published. It's filled with heart-wrenching case histories and juicy glimpses into the intimate lives of real men and women who faced personal crises. We're told about the life-altering choices they made and the repercussions of those choices for the generations that followed. We read how they coped, what worked for them (and what didn't), the behaviors that led to destruction, and what changes brought success and lasting happiness. Interventions and dramas abound. One thing sets this book apart from the others. It includes our Creator's perspective.

31

Were the people profiled in the Bible different from us? What must it have been like for those who were privileged to spend time with the greatest man this world has ever known – to be chosen to travel with Jesus, sit around a campfire with Him, witness His miracles, listen to Him teach, hear Him pray, laugh and cry? Only stories frozen on thin, gilded pages speak for His companions now. What would they say to us today if they were here?

Over the centuries these very human men and women have been cloaked in religious glamour and awarded super-saint status. I doubt any of them thought they deserved a pedestal. They were ordinary people, and to forget that is to overlook an important aspect of their legacies. Our Creator knows that each of our different personalities will learn in its own way. When we take time to look deeper, we see parts of ourselves reflected in our spiritual ancestors, and hear them speak to us. Our Lord befriended them just as they were, for He knew who they would become. He has chosen each of us in the same way.

Some of us are like Peter – full of contradictions – proud, stubborn, passionate, impetuous, strong, weak. We like to be the boss and are prone to forgetting that *we* aren't in charge – the Master is. We have learned the hard way that the question: *"How does one become humble?"* can be answered, *"By being humiliated."* But each time we stumble and fall, we'll get back up wiser, stronger and more empowered than before – and the Lord knew from the beginning that eventually *"...the reed would turn into a rock"* upon which He could build.

Matthew 14:27-31 • John 13-6-9 • John 6:66-69 • Matthew 26:69-7

Is there any of Zacchaeus in those who love the comfort of wealth and position, who hide behind credentials and are proud of their worldly success? Isn't it obvious, yet, that none of our striving can add even one inch to our small stature? Would we be seen climbing a tree in a business suit so as to catch a glimpse of a homeless itinerant preacher walking by? How would we answer if he spotted us and invited himself to dinner at our house in the suburbs? And how would we respond when he showed up with a bunch of his homeless friends in tow?

Would all of our misplaced priorities shuffle into order when He looked straight through our façade and we saw in His eyes, eternal riches that made all of our possessions look like junk? Perhaps, it would dawn on us then, that *we* are the poor. • *Luke 19:1-10*

W hat would happen if no one was like Martha? (I'm referring to Martha, the sister of Mary and Lazarus, not the well-known domestic diva by the same name, though their skills were no doubt similar). Would there ever again be dinner parties? Who would manage, organize, shop, decorate, entertain and serve with efficiency and style, while graciously declining all praise with a casual wave and *"Oh, it was nothing..."*? Would the less-gifted just have to muddle through somehow without instruction? In all of the planning and *busy*-ness, the joy of simplicity and spontaneity can be forgotten. Thoughtfulness can turn into bossiness and caring can become control. When we expect approval and appreciation for martyring ourselves to keep everyone else happy, we're bound to feel angry and resentful when they take us for granted instead.

The battle cry of a "Martha" is, *"Well, who's going to do it if I don't?"* Life is exhausting when *doing* is more important than *being*. Precious moments drown in the stormy sea of stress. Jesus Himself might be out in the living room waiting to talk to us if we would ever come out of the kitchen, but we're in there rattling dishes, grumbling because Mary isn't helping, frantically making coffee, and worrying about whether we'll have enough cookies for everybody who showed up without an invitation to sit at the Lord's feet. • *Luke 10:38-42*

W e are all like the blind man, the leper, Job, and Lazarus, dead in his tomb – helpless against this flesh until the power of the Spirit moves through our bodies and minds, heals us, changes us and gives us a new life. We are captives of darkness, tormented by our demons, until the light of truth dispels the shadows and sets us free.

John 9 • *Matthew 21:30-34; 8:1-3* • *The Book of Job* • *John 11:17-45* • *Matthew 17:14-2*

W e are the thieves on either side of Christ's cross – deserving of our punishment for the sins we commit. Yet some will argue viewpoints with their dying breaths. He offers us absolution from the highest court and we, the accused, are left with the choice to accept it or not. In the end, each one of us must decide for ourselves if the man hanging between us is who He says He is. • *Luke 23:33-43*

There are parts of these people in all of us, but one woman's passion is mine. Braving the scorn of those she knew would judge her, she fell to her knees and washed her Lord's feet with tears that flowed from the well of a soul He had cleansed with forgiveness. He was different than anyone she'd ever known, and the only man who had ever seen her heart. His understanding had given her the power to change her life, and what anyone else thought about her would never matter again. It was enough that Jesus knew who she was – and loved her.

"A woman knew Jesus was having dinner in a Pharisee's house. She brought an alabaster box of ointment and weeping, began to wash His feet with tears and wiped them with her hair, and poured the ointment on them. The Pharisee saw it and mumbled, 'If this man really was a prophet, he'd know what kind of a woman this is and he'd never let her touch him.' Jesus heard him and said, 'Her sins, which are many, are forgiven, so she loves much. Those who think they need little forgiveness love little." And he said to her, 'Your faith has saved you. Go in peace."

Luke 7:37-50

34

Entwined

By God's design we were one for a time
before years, miles, and opposing views
opened a chasm between our hearts.
Trust slid into the rift,
our arms reached for one another from far away,
but our lips seldom spoke the words we both needed to hear.

After so long
how could we not have known one another better?
Or did we know each other too well to tell
the forest from the trees?
Was objectivity an impossibility?

Our lovely masks fooled other eyes,
smiles hid the pain inside.
Defensive, indignant, denying our sins,
we cast deadly stones and torched fragile bridges
with words that burned
until there was nothing left to say
that we hadn't both already heard.

We walked, after that, each of us alone,
through our own valleys and fires.
You warned me of the day I'd understand...
'Twas a place you knew better than I...
but I had to travel there by myself,
and when I arrived, you had already gone on ahead.

Oh, Mama ... my eyes could only be my own.

I longed to reassure you,

to solve the sorrows and struggles,
to vanquish your fears and grief.
Could my own pain balance the scales?
Would you know, then, that I understood?

I felt you bleed,

you tasted my tears,
as we clung to Forgiveness' battered breast
again
and again.

*T*oo early, too young

you left this world fighting, as always.
I waged faith's war with you to the end ~
no other way to atone for the days
of my childish, selfish anger and blame.
You had no strength left to utter absolution
nor to lay a blessing upon my head,
God gave you release
from pain to peace,
and off you ran through Heaven's door
without even a sweet "Good-bye."

I built a shrine in my heart,

crowned you with sainthood,
placed precious mementos everywhere.
Cherished fragments of your life,
the trinkets you touched,
the pearls you wore,
your blissful face in a frame,
cradling your baby girl.

I sanctified the altar with my tears,
wore it smooth with prayers of penance over the years,
until the day
you took me by surprise!

The unmistakable fragrance
of your love filled the room,
and my soul held it's breath in wonder...
embraced, enthralled, I listened,
as you spoke to me in a song.

You said you knew I needed you
and that you would always be near,
"When you are weak, I will be strong,
helping you to carry on."
I ached to trust your healing words
but old doubts shook their heads.
You saw them and whispered you understood,
but that everything had changed.

"*In* Heaven's halls we wrote our pact,
and perfect love has brought me back
to ask if you can release me yet
from those painful years in the flesh.
They're over now, their lessons learned,
and I've been redeemed, you see."

Scars vanished today
when you lifted the veil
and I recognized your perfect soul!
My sister, my mother, companion and teacher,
my faithful, eternal friend.
In a twinkling I'll be there with you again ~
not missing you so
not letting you go...

37

In love's pure light...

Entwined.

In loving, joyful memory of Katiza Tomich, my Mother

Cinderella

I know it's time to walk with You,

my Beloved,
and if I ever needed to,
it's now.
But I can't stand in Your holy light
dressed in these dirty rags.

You see, someone held up a mirror today,

pointed out my obvious unworthiness,
said they were an authority,
and that sins such as mine could not just disappear
like magic.

They knew Your words so well!

Spliced them into ropes that bound ~
wielded them like weapons to wound ~
recited the rules ~
said I still owed dues ~
patted me on the head
and left me here alone
in ashes.

Your eyes will see my soul.

I want to hide from what I know is there
and from You.
But You know me so well, and where I will go ~
wherever I turn, You're already there waiting.

And so I will come as I am ~ broken ~
into the light that exposes truth and lies.

You are there,
waiting to brush away my tears ~
longing to dress me in the riches
of your grace.

I surrender.

The rags vanish.

The slipper fits.

You smile,
hold out Your hand,
the music begins
and we dance.

"This then is how we know that we belong to the Truth, and how we set our
hearts at rest in His presence whenever our hearts condemn us. For God is
greater than our hearts, and He knows everything."
•
I John 3:19-20

"...to give to them that mourn...beauty for ashes, the oil of joy for mourning, the
garment of praise for the spirit of heaviness..."
•
Isaiah 61:1-3

SAMARITAN

I never knew your name
but I remember the humility in your soft, sad eyes.
Brother of Christ, forgive those who turn away –
they have not walked the city streets in your worn out shoes.
I won't pretend I don't see you there
praying for a meal and a bed.

I'll never find out how you came to your plight
for we didn't have time to talk today.
I was running behind schedule, you see.
I'd overslept beneath my warm comforter,
and by the time I got up, had my latté, ate breakfast, took a hot shower,
dressed in my freshly pressed suit, kissed my loving family good-bye,
and jumped behind the wheel of my shiny new car,
I was quite late for the shareholders' meeting.

I saw you standing at the crossroads
wrapped in a ragged blanket against the chill.
The light changed and I saw you again,
curled up on a park bench,
huddled in a doorway,
waiting, weeping on the Mission steps.
And as I passed, you asked me if I could help.

Something in your thankful smile was so familiar –
as though we'd met before.
I have so much – and I did so little
I wish I'd had more time to stay – to help you more.
"God Bless You,"
The words came from your heart, as did mine:
"God bless you, too."
And I hurried on my way.

Two souls –
One poor, one rich –
and only their Father
knows which is which.

ॐ

"...in as much as you have done it unto the least of these, my brothers, you have done it unto me." ◆ Jesus, Matthew 25:34-40

"...the rich and poor meet together: the Lord is the maker of them all."
◆ Proverbs 22:2

"...so laboring you ought to support the weak, remembering the words of Jesus, that it is more blessed to give than receive." ◆ Acts 20:35

Jesus' Parable of the Good Samaritan ◆ Luke 10:30-37

"Blessed are the poor in spirit, for theirs is the kingdom of heaven.
Blessed are those who mourn, for they will be comforted.
Blessed are the meek, for they will inherit the earth.
Blessed are those who hunger and thirst for righteousness,
for they will be filled.
Blessed are the merciful, for they will be shown mercy." ◆ Matthew 5:3-7

"For you know the grace of our Lord Jesus Christ, that though He was rich, yet for your sakes He became poor, so that you through His poverty might become rich." ◆ II Corinthians 8:9

"Instruct those who are rich in this present world not to be conceited, nor to fix their hope on the uncertainty of riches, but on God, who richly supplies us with all things to enjoy. Instruct them to be rich in good deeds, and to be generous and willing to share." ◆ I Timothy 6:17-18

TRUTH and CONSEQUENCES

We seek to hear truth, but many different voices insist they have it, and versions vary drastically. Can there be more than one truth?

The flesh might answer this way: *"I don't really know or care. Just give me what makes me feel good for the time being, and I'll call that my truth."*

Intellect may deliberate: *"I need to think about that, gather data, analyze it, and arrive at a logical conclusion."*

But Spirit will say: *"Truth? When I hear it, I will know it."*

The different aspects of our being are often in conflict with one another, leaving us confused and frustrated. We crave balance between the three, but it's an ongoing, painstaking process to achieve it.

Truth is a gem with many different facets, but at its core, there is only *"I Am."* It presents itself in unexpected moments, in unlikely places, through unlikely sources, and is revealed only when we are open and seeking it. Like flakes of gold in the sand, we happen upon it one small particle at a time. The wise collect these, for they add up.

Truth is an unfolding mystery. We must find and fit together the clues. It often keeps silence in the direct line of questioning, and if we do get an answer, it can cut to the heart like a double-edged sword. Truth seekers are spared nothing. The first time we find ourselves holding the severed remains of one of our favorite sacred cows, it's traumatic indeed...but if we are brave enough to continue our quest, God will teach us – one lesson at a time – how to wield the sword of truth ourselves.

The foregoing speaks to spiritual truth but we must deal with physical realities, too. It's a challenge to discern the truth under one's own roof, let alone in our neighborhood, our country and our world. In fact, it seems impossible. But God does not want His children to live in ignorance. When we ask Him, He will reveal all of the truths we seek, and I've had many occasions to put that to the test.

"Lord, I ask that You cause the truth to be revealed to me in this situation," is a powerful prayer when we are in doubt or confusion, and it has *never* failed to bring results for me. God has answered in some creative ways, and more than once, as I squirmed, I've heard Him say, *"Well, if you didn't want to know, you shouldn't have asked!"*

If we'd rather cower in the darkness of denial, He'll let us stay there. But if we are brave enough to face cold, hard facts when He shines the light on them, then He can lead us out.

For a good many years of my life, an ever-growing mountain of heartbreaks made me suspicious that I was getting more than my fair share of tribulation. I was repeatedly taken advantage of, lied to, swindled and betrayed and I began to fear I must be missing some vital spiritual tool that others with fewer problems seemed to possess. Why did my good-hearted trust always turn out to be misplaced? Was I dumb? Naïve? Was there a target on my forehead? While I was preoccupied pouring out unconditional love, others were busy plotting my downfall. *Why didn't I ever see it coming?*

For a time, I adopted the notion that my suffering was "for righteousness sake," and therefore, somehow glorious. This – and my short-lived attempt at silent martyrdom (the art form practiced by more-experienced sufferers) – did no more than cast a dark cloud over everyone in proximity. As laughing comes more naturally to me than wallowing in misery, you can imagine my relief in being able to abandon the latter when my Heavenly Father informed me, one fine day, that it was *good* for me to be happy and He preferred to see me that way.

I still needed to fix my problem, though, so my next survival tactic was to keep to myself. I reasoned that if I didn't get involved with others, I could avoid trouble. If I never put my heart on the line, nobody could squash it. If I never trusted completely, no one could deceive me. I wasn't going to risk being hurt again like in the past, nor did I need to repeat any of the painful lessons I'd already learned. I wasn't keen on being presented with any *new* learning opportunities, either. Not if they were going to hurt as much as the previous bunch had. If pain was the teacher, I wasn't going to class. I refer to those as the "desert years." Like Moses, I adapted to the wilderness and became quite content.

Throughout all that time I always consistently and desperately prayed that God would bestow upon me greater wisdom, discernment and insight so that I could be alerted to pitfalls and not blunder into bad situations. I knew He wanted me to walk boldly in love and power, but I didn't trust myself not to make more disastrous, emotionally-costly mistakes.

Perhaps it took that period of self-imposed seclusion for me to finally be able to receive the understanding I so desperately needed, but I remember the day that it came. Another dilemma had arisen and I had been moaning my same old worn-out prayer. *"Oh, God, I ask You to give me discernment in this situation! I need it so bad!"*

God's response was immediate, and I can only describe His tone as "long-suffering." I was so shocked – and so relieved – that I didn't know whether to laugh or cry. I think I did both.

"How long are you going to beg Me for discernment!? I gave it to you long ago the first time you asked. The problem is that you argue with it!"

After so very long, I'd finally been able to hear His answer, and any excuse or attempt at denial was futile. The flashbacks began, and I saw that I had *always* been given warnings when a situation wasn't right – an uncomfortable feeling, concerned input from others, or obvious road blocks, to name just a few. God had *always* waved the red flag, and sometimes *many* flags, in plenty of time for me to slow down and avoid disaster, but I had rationalized, pushed aside and rejected that discernment in action. I'd argued with it when heeding the warnings meant STOP, and had kept my foot on the accelerator instead. I'd doubted the cautioning voice if obedience meant my own agenda would have to be disrupted, postponed or abandoned. When hearing *"No"* would have brought disappointment or the relinquishing of expectations, I'd plugged my ears. I'd put discernment off when I felt uncomfortable or timid about confronting someone with facts, or when I was more concerned about sparing their feelings than speaking truth. And I'd ignored it while I stubbornly persisted in protecting or romanticizing people or situations when my Father wanted to "call game" and reveal the truth. He'd tried to spare me every single time, but I'd wanted my own way.

I've argued with the voice of discernment for a multitude of reasons in the past, but I don't doubt it anymore. Even when I can't pinpoint the reason for an uncomfortable twinge in the pit of my stomach that's telling me something isn't quite right, I pay heed to that feeling and wait until more is revealed. I don't care, anymore, what I may risk by putting on the brakes or changing direction. I know I can't ever see the whole picture nor can I know what is in the hearts of others. Only God knows, and I count myself very fortunate if He's willing to clue me in when I ask.

These words, spoken by Dan Korem – an investigative reporter/profiler and inspirational speaker – changed my life:

"Love the truth more than you fear your pain and you'll be a hard person to fool."

Oh, what freedom those words can bring, and how often I have clung to them! When we find the courage to reach for and embrace truth, regardless of the pain it may bring, we *eliminate* the prolonged agony we would otherwise endure while trying, in vain, to prevent the inevitable. When truth is ugly, we don't want to acknowledge it or deal with it. We'd rather avoid it, hold it at arm's length and fight it off. We turn away, make excuses, and hope it will be proven false. If it is attached to something we're heavily vested in, we *want* to go into denial. And, sadly, we're capable of deceiving ourselves interminably.

But truth does not go away. Ever. It continues, relentlessly, to manifest and prove itself – and we need never be left in doubt.

Deception – whichever end of it you are on – has consequences, and so does truth. Both sets of repercussions can be painful, but the former bind and destroy while the latter liberate and empower. These days I bow to truth more quickly and experience greater peace as a result. I used to fear that I could not endure the disillusionment, disappointment, pain or loss that some truths might bring if I looked them square in the face. My fears were unfounded, for they insinuate that we can trust our Father to sustain and carry us through some things, but not all.

The pain that accompanied some truths did not kill or cripple me. In fact, when I lowered my defenses and let it in, it hurt far less than I'd feared and imagined. It washed over me like a wave, but I did not drown, and survived to live and love more wisely than before. Over and over throughout my life I have seen irrefutable proof that we are the children of a *loving* God who will bring us through the darkest night and heal the deepest wounds when we allow Him to be active in our lives. He is the Giver of Truth and He wants us to seek it from Him.

Philosophies, beliefs and information can be passed on, shared and taught, but no one can call Truth his or her own without first experiencing the longing, turmoil, pain and joy of its birth within his or her own heart.

❧ *John 8:32* ☙

These Eyes

I thought I heard You say,

"Open your eyes"
but I questioned the Voice
that never lies.
Days passed by,
Your words remained,
I pondered their meaning,
it was simple, the same.

These eyes have seen sorrow, betrayal and pain...

blinded by tears, I closed them again.
Into the darkness I walked by feel,
followed the sounds people made...
thought I could tell,
but I stumbled and fell,
and from my fear I prayed.

For these eyes love the stars

and the fresh, shining dream,
passion's innocent image on a soul washed clean.
These eyes seek to read others',
long to trust, laugh, unveil,
seek wisdom, discernment, and cry when they fail.
These eyes search for light
beyond rain clouds that sigh,
scan hope's shadowed horizons
where roads of change lie.

What is imagined?

What is real?
Aren't we more
than that which we feel?

Rose-colored glasses spare us the gray,
paint ugliness lovely,
I've cast them away.
Steps measured cautious, now
toward the goal,
obstacles clearer,
let the journey unfold.

Eyes wiser now,

yet still those of the child,
open to truth — undefiled.
It was always there,
it does not hide...
What courage it takes

To look inside.

♦

THE SOURCE

My friend, Anne, was writing a book and I'd offered to help with the manuscript. After several attempts to work at home failed, it became clear that without a longer stretch of quiet, uninterrupted time, we weren't going to make much progress. We talked wistfully of how much we'd be able to accomplish if we could manage a weekend away, but there was no allowance in our budgets for such a luxury.

A few days later, our wish came up in a conversation Anne was having with a small group of ladies, and to her surprise, one of the women made a generous offer. Her family's cabin at a lake resort up toward the mountain was unoccupied much of the winter, and we were welcome to use it for a weekend. Anne happily accepted on the spot. We shuffled schedules, marked our calendars, and arranged for the bases to be covered on our respective home fronts in our absence.

Midday on a Friday, we waved good-bye to our clans and headed for the foothills as fast as two working mothers could escape in a station wagon. The cold gray skies and unrelenting drizzle couldn't dampen our spirits, and we filled the long drive with chatter and cheery plans for the next two Heaven-sent days.

Our hostess had described the cabin as *"...cute and cozy...rustic and charming."* Ahhh...peace and quiet at last! We imagined how we'd snuggle down in overstuffed chairs and sip steaming mugs of spiced tea in front of a toasty fire...and work on Anne's book of course, since that was the excuse for our weekend retreat.

As we neared our destination, the heavens opened and Washington State's famous liquid sunshine poured down from above. Visibility became poor, so we stopped at a small store to confirm our directions. The craggy owner raised a wiry quizzical eyebrow at the word "resort," before pointing us onward *"...about four miles on yer right, ya can't miss it."* We jumped back in the car and headed down the home stretch, filled with anticipation and excitement...until we spotted the entrance.

Our happy bubble splattered like one of the gigantic raindrops pounding the windshield, and our groans of disappointment were swept just as dispassionately aside by the frantically-slapping wipers. With trepidation, we turned in and slowed to the crawl commanded by a handmade sign nailed to a tree. The area had been logged, and the

49

narrow gravel road that wound down through the remaining scraggly trees was etched with deep ruts and potholes. Peering through the rain-streaked car windows, we searched for the cabin amongst others which looked – judging from the 4x4 trucks and large, salivating dogs that loudly announced our arrival – to be year-round dwellings.

Nine... ten... eleven... and there it was: Number Twelve (in reflective golden digits above the door).

There was no lake in sight, and our surroundings quelled any desire to investigate. It was almost dark and we were tired and hungry. We briefly considered scrapping our plans, but knowing that another weekend furlough was unlikely to present itself again any time soon, we decided to stay and make the best of the situation.

Parking strategically so that we could straddle the mud puddles, we unloaded the groceries, typewriter and suitcases onto the porch. Then, we braced ourselves, coaxed the key into the padlock, opened the door, and stepped inside. One look around was the final death blow to our unrealistic expectations for a lovely weekend.

The place was cold, damp, and smelled like a combination of mildew and the last trout fry of the summer. Heat and lights were our first order of business, but when we flipped the switch by the door, nothing happened. Our next hope was a dusty wicker swag lamp hanging from the ceiling. We rolled the switch on the cord, the light came on, and for a brief second in the warmth of its glow, the room was a friendlier place. Then, with a loud pop and sizzle, the bulb exploded, spewing sparks into the tinder-dry cage and igniting it like a tiki torch.

As the fixture blazed overhead, we ran around in frantic circles trying to remember the protocol for an electrical fire and desperately searching for something other than our coats to smother the flames. By the time I found two old towels in the bathroom, the flaming basket was dangling precariously from its melted cord. With no time to lose, we threw the towels on top and it crashed to the floor, disintegrating upon impact into countless fiery tidbits of red-hot wicker that skittered with deadly speed and purpose across the old wood planks and threadbare scatter rugs.

Pandemonium ensued as we chased, pounced and stomped on the small infernos until we'd finally extinguished all of them. Then, tragedy narrowly averted, we looked at each other in stunned disbelief and burst into uncontrollable laughter.

After sobering up, we took stock of the sooty mess. The main light source was toast, smoke filled the cabin, and the only two towels in residence were now scorched and covered with soot. Whatever evil forces had concocted this welcome fiasco were in for a surprise. We were combat-hardened mommies who dealt with sibling warfare, broken bones, head wounds and 80 mph trips to the emergency room on a regular basis. Compared to an average day with our kids, this was still a stroll in the park.

We opened a window to clear out the smoke and began the quest for heat. Spying a rusty baseboard heater under the front window, we crossed our fingers and cranked the dial. It retaliated with ghostly noises and an odd smell, so given our earlier misadventure, we immediately turned it back off. The little potbelly stove in the corner looked equally untrustworthy, but it didn't really matter one way or the other, because our search for matches, newspapers, kindling or firewood also proved futile. After more discussion, we decided it was time to call the owners and ask them what to do. This assumed that the phone worked, which of course, it did not. *(Author's note: We had no cell phones, laptops or email in those days!)*

The discovery that one burner on the kitchen stove actually worked was cause for rejoicing, and we immediately filled a pan with water for much-needed instant coffee. Then we donned several layers of clothing, shoved all the furniture toward the only functioning electrical outlet, plugged in the typewriter and a small table lamp, and determined that a sense of humor was going to be our best hope for the weekend ahead. Fortunately, that was a gift we'd always activated in one another whenever we were together.

In spite of everything, we made quite a bit of progress that evening, and it was past midnight when we rolled out our sleeping bags on the moist mattresses in the loft, where we giggled and talked for another hour like adolescents at a slumber party.

By morning, the rain had stopped and things seemed more tolerable. The hours flew by as I typed while Anne dictated, and we were surprised when the daylight began to fade. (Northwest folk cope with the dreaded stretch of short winter days in different ways, hibernation being the preferred method, aided by a measure of denial. It isn't unusual to hear us exclaim, *"I do not believe it's actually getting dark at four o'clock in the afternoon!"* as though we are witnessing unnatural

51

phenomena. In the woods, beneath a thick layer of rain clouds, four o'clock becomes three.)

The lights in the cabin flickered sporadically as they'd done the night before, convincing us that the wiring was faulty and that the walls might begin to smolder at any moment. The large, wolfish dog next door began barking incessantly and others joined in. No one quieted them – probably because they'd trained them to scare off prowlers, bear, cougar, Bigfoot (a local legend and popular theme for our famed chainsaw carvers) or worse. We didn't know who might have seen us arrive, and the closest pay phone was many miles away. Our uneasiness grew and concentration became impossible, so we decided to take a break.

Anne went to the kitchen, and I walked into the bathroom, where I turned on the faucet and waited for the hot water to arrive. An old medicine cabinet hung on the wall above the sink, and while I thawed my cold hands beneath the welcome flow of warm water, I gazed into the corroded mirror on its door. To my wonderment, in place of my reflection, a vision began to form.

Surrounded by the darkness of space, a magnificent, shining orb of massive proportions appeared. It pulsed and churned with vibrant, oscillating colors and bursts of energy that were released in flashes of brilliant light. I was mesmerized, and could not take my eyes from its incredible power and beauty.

Billions of living, moving threads completely covered the orb's exterior. They were a part of it as well as conduits for the energy. The power flowed into and through these channels and was then directed out into the universe. Throughout this process, the tremendous energy being generated by the orb was never diminished. As I tried to grasp what I was seeing, I was given the knowledge that the orb was *the Source of life.*

I felt an intense desire to see the orb in greater detail, and immediately, as though in response, the picture "zoomed in," allowing me to see the individual strands. While many were healthy, strong, and pulsing with light, others were crimped, twisted and unhealthy in appearance, causing them to be dim, shadowed, or dark within. Although the light and energy poured from the orb equally into every strand at their points of connection, these life forces were prevented from passing completely through the darkened ones. It seemed that if the bruised, knotted strands remained in that condition for a long time, they might begin to die for lack of the energy that needed to be flowing through them. When I pondered this, I was given the understanding that because they were a part of it, The Source could feel their pain. I saw the flow of power continuously attempt to get through these channels, and although it was constricted somewhat by the bruises – where it appeared to gather and linger – it completely stopped when it reached a knot.

As I continued to absorb the vision, fuller understanding came. Had I never been shown any other spiritual pictures in my life; nor ever heard any other truth from God; nor ever read His words on a page; nor ever felt Him teach and comfort my heart, this *one* revelation would have been enough for a lifetime – and indeed, it has been – *for God was showing me who we really are.*

Our soul's birthplace is one of unimaginable glory. Every unique soul is a child of Father God, Who is The Source of all power, light and love. We are siblings – all eternally part of the whole and therefore part of one another. Each of us has been endowed with and equally possesses the ability to receive and conduct the attributes of the vast resources to which we are connected. Our Father not only desires to channel those energies through us, but this flow is *essential,* for it is the nature of that omnipotent power to pour forth, not to be contained. Its force is far too mighty to be held back or held within.

I saw healthy, glowing souls who were transmitting light effortlessly. Some of these appeared to be fuller and stronger, as though they had been stretched to accommodate a greater volume. But regardless of their varying sizes, all the channels that were filled with light were vibrant, flexible, healthy and beautiful, and they functioned together in perfect harmony, none overshadowing another.

Suddenly, the human quest for the roots of our being made perfect sense, as did the search for our relationship to God, the mystery of our purpose here, and our sense that there is more that we are capable of giving and receiving than what we often experience.

Next, I was shown that the souls who shared the same attributes in that spiritual existence would recognize one another when they encountered one another in the course of a human lifetime, and that this could bring them much joy and strength. I thought about Anne in the other room, and the bond we'd felt from the moment we met. Scriptures that speak of eternal connection sprang to mind, and took on new meaning.

"...If I say, 'Surely the darkness will hide me and the light become night around me,' even the darkness will not be dark to You; the night will shine like the day...For You created my inmost being; You knit

me together in my mother's womb...When I was made in the secret place...woven together in the depths of the earth, Your eyes saw my unformed body. All the days ordained for me were written in Your book before one of them came to be." • Psalm 139

And Jesus' words: *"Inasmuch as you have done it unto the least of these my brothers, you have done it unto me."* • Matthew 25:40

In response to my concern for the shadowed souls, I was shown that they were suffering for lack of the power that was intended to flow through them, and that only the same loving energy could heal them. It seemed as though the bruises had not necessarily been their own doing, and that the warmth of the light would erase these in time if they allowed it to enter and remained yielded to it. The knots, however, had been self-inflicted. The souls had twisted themselves into these painful positions by harboring un-forgiveness, anger, bitterness, fear, judgment and other negative attitudes, and now those things were choking and crippling them. The longer they held on to them, the tighter the knots grew. Only they, themselves, could release and undo them. When they chose to do so, the light would once again be able to enter, bringing healing with it.

I saw that the souls surrounding them were affected by their suffering, and that their instinct was to support the weaker or wounded ones and radiate warmth to them. But it was made clear to me that although the power was available to all, the responsibility rested solely on each individual to open themselves as a channel. In doing so, their distinct, individual purpose could be fulfilled. One could never do this for another. It was not anatomically possible in the spiritual sense.

In a few moments, the vision faded away, leaving me to marvel at what I'd seen. I turned off the water and walked back out into the living room. The picture filled my mind, and I did not know how I could possibly describe it to Anne. Would she think I'd gone crazy? We always shared everything with one another, and I didn't know how I could keep this to myself. I looked at her and noticed she seemed a bit distracted. I assumed she was still unsettled by the dogs – or worse yet, maybe the kitchen stove had stopped working.

Hesitantly, I began. *"Uh...Annie...you're probably going to think this is really strange, but just now when I was in the bathroom...I... I saw this ...well...I'd have to call it a vision, I guess...and it was the most beautiful, incredible thing..."* I began gesturing in the air but before I got very far her jaw dropped and she interrupted me in an incredulous voice. *"You saw it too!?"* Then she attempted her own description.

54

Though it was impossible for either of us to adequately convey what we'd seen, there was no doubt that we'd both been given the same revelation – a fact that only added to our amazement. It seemed God had done this to abolish any doubts that might have arisen in either of our minds otherwise. What the Holy Spirit had revealed was so clear and simple that it would have been impossible to misconstrue it, but we both knew that some teachings within our religious backgrounds would clash with such an image of the Creator and us, His children souls. Within those sacred moments, our previous understanding of our relationship to God had not only been vastly expanded, but in some respects altered completely.

As we pondered and discussed the vision, the atmosphere in the room slowly began to change and we became attuned to an energy we hadn't noticed before. It continued to intensify until the air was almost crackling with electricity – and this time the cabin's wiring was not a factor. Something supernatural was taking place.

Outside, the dogs continued to bark, and inside the lights flickered. We agreed that we had just been shown the kind of power that could flow through us if we allowed it to. We knew, now, that we were conduits of that energy and could direct it. It surrounded us, and we sensed we were being given the opportunity to test our new understanding. What were we waiting for? Were we afraid we'd look silly? To whom? We looked at each other and said, *"Why not?"*

Speaking together out loud, we focused and released the energy, and felt it rush forth, invincible in its power to accomplish what we wanted it to. *"Dogs...peace! Be still!"*

The frenzied barking *instantly* ceased and there was silence. Astonished, we looked at one another. Was this what happened when Jesus calmed the storm? The energy felt invincible, and we knew it was ours to channel at will. It seemed logical to direct it toward the cabin's electrical issues next, so we did that, too. The lights stopped flickering and there were no more problems for the remainder of our stay.

All the power of the universe is at our fingertips – literally! Why don't we use it? Bruises, knots, insecurities, selfishness, fear, ignorance, stubbornness – why do we allow the holding of these sad, painful things to clog the healing flow that is waiting to surge through us? We must guard against anyone or anything that attempts to condemn, control, complicate or confuse our hearts or minds. We've been sold the lie that we are impotent and unworthy, that we have little or nothing to offer, and that we are separated and cut off from our Creator and left here to struggle on our own. *Nothing could be further from the truth!*

Anne and I have never forgotten that weekend or the greater purpose for which we were sent to that humble little cabin. We have since both been given many opportunities to share the Holy Spirit's message with others so that they can know they are eternally connected to The Source of all love, life and power, and that their purpose is simply to stay open to the flow of that omnipotent energy.

We are all One, having been given life by a common Parent whose attributes we share. When we acknowledge the kinship and equality of all souls, we will instinctively extend warmth and support to our brothers and sisters who are struggling or suffering. When we accept their individuality, we will allow each their own unique expression.

We can *all*, without exception, discover the joy of Divine power flowing through the distinct channel we were each born to be. This is our Creator's desire. If we are bruised, we will be healed. If we cannot feel the life-force that should be ours beyond a certain point, we should check for knots. If they are found, we need only relax and do whatever it takes to untie them so that God's Spirit can flow through us to others, uninhibited and pure. It will cleanse us as it does.

We are channels of power, light and love. In this lies the purpose of our existence.

Many years have passed since that weekend, but not a day has gone by that I haven't remembered the vision. Once, while I was meditating upon it during a walk, God interrupted me with a question, which He asked me to answer with the Holy Spirit's reasoning rather than my own. I sensed this was because someone *else* was going to ask me the question, and He wanted me to be prepared.

The question was this: *"If your souls are eternally joined to Me, why do you need a Savior?"*

I stopped dead in my tracks. Why, indeed? There's no question that *I* need a Savior, but scores of people claim to be fine without one, and many of them are good-hearted, loving people who lead unselfish lives of service. I walked another three miles pondering the answer to God's question and asking the Holy Spirit for understanding and the words to express it.

Jesus came to earth from the heart of God to remind us of who we are: His brothers and sisters. He became human and lived amongst us to show us the purpose of *our* human existence. He put eternal truths into words so that upon hearing them, our souls would reawaken and we would remember where we came from and where we are going. He taught us how to commune with our Father, how to love one another, how to heal and be healed, and in all of His words and deeds He became our example of how to live during the time we are given on this earth.

Our Mentor knows the predispositions of the human form and that these can war with our spirits while we dwell in these bodies. He does not judge us, but instead offers to continuously cleanse and redeem us when our thoughts and deeds contaminate us. According to our willingness, He illuminates our hearts and minds so we can recognize our higher calling and follow it.   • John 1:1-3

From beginning to end, Jesus' human life fulfilled the Messianic prophecies of the ages. He possessed the power to spare himself unspeakable agony, yet He allowed His body to be crucified. He carried the crushing burden of our condemnation with Him to the cross so that we'd be spared. His sacrifice was a demonstration of the ultimate triumph of spirit over flesh, love over hate, forgiveness over punishment and eternal life over death. Because He knew human minds could not fathom this, He asked us to accept it by faith, as little children, and to look at His miracles as proof of His sovereignty. • Matthew 11:1-5

Jesus came to save us from being overtaken by the nature of the bodies our spirits inhabit while on earth, and to empower us so we can overcome the evil that coexists with us here.   Only our spirits can recognize The Christ. *"Therefore, I want you to understand that no one speaking by the Spirit of God ever says, 'Jesus be cursed!' and no one can say 'Jesus is Lord,' except by the Holy Spirit."* • I Corinthians 12:3 This was true even before He was born. Some souls recognize Him sooner than others, but all souls will see Him again and will then know, without question or debate, Who He was, is, and always will be.

The answer to the question is this:
We need a Savior to rescue us from drowning in this humanness.
Jesus is that gift.

෨

57

S. G. Rose

58

COMMISSION

Spirit challenged to live in flesh, foreign foe…
what I brought here I give,
released, I will go.
Reaching to touch, other hearts await…
I lay down my love – by choice, by fate.
Spread out the table with all I possess,
others take what they're able,
I cannot offer less.
Wandering eyes have not seen my soul,
minds yet shrouded, survival their goal.

I salvage gems from the ashes of loss
but the One Whom I follow
never counted the cost.
When the stars sang and life was new
with passion I cried, *"Let me follow You!"*
He held out His hand, I ran to His side,
then Love broke my heart
when I saw how He'd died.

Shades and stages of letting go…
storm that rages – here, it must be so.
Tears last but a season, only faith's eyes can see
through shadows of reason
why each cross needs to be.

I shall stay strong
for the task is not done…
all I need, I was given
when I chose to come.

◆

Surely the Lord God
does nothing
without revealing His secret
to His servants, the prophets.
The lion has roared;
who will not fear?
The Lord God has spoken;
who can but prophesy?

Amos 3:7-8

Messages

While most often thought of as the foretelling of events, that which we call prophesy is also sent from God for comfort, encouragement and guidance.

"Follow the way of love and eagerly desire spiritual gifts, especially the gift of prophesy. For...everyone who prophesies speaks to men for their strengthening, encouragement and comfort."

•

I Corinthians 14:1,3

When such a message forms in the heart with the sense that it is meant to be shared, that commission carries with it the gravest of all responsibilities. I believe it would be better for someone who claims they have heard from God to literally choke on the words should they not really be from Him, than to speak idly and have to give account to the Almighty later for misrepresentation.

"The fear of the Lord is the beginning of wisdom" • Psalm 111:10

Tragically, there are many self-appointed prophets and sooth-sayers out there with a variety of motives who seem to have no qualms about speaking on God's behalf. They obviously do not share my fear of the consequences should it turn out they are wrong and have led those who believed them astray. • Matthew 18:6

We have countless questions for our Heavenly Father, and He invites us to ask them. Sometimes, his reply is "Trust Me," wrapped in silence. But how exciting it is when answers come! I will never forget the first time it happened to me. With childlike glee I shared my experience with the wrong person (we'll call her "Helga"). Admittedly, I was young and naïve back then, and put my head on the block by blurting out something like, *"You'll never believe what God told me yesterday!"*

Helga glared at me incredulously and cut me down with one ruthless sentence: *"What gives you the audacity to think that God would speak to you!?"*

I squirmed like a worm on a hook. Seeing she'd hit an artery, Helga temporarily sheathed her dagger and took pity on me. In a firm, authoritative tone, as though she were rebuking the village idiot, she explained why I needed to *stop* the crazy talk. God, in case I didn't know, had already communicated everything He wanted known through those who wrote the Bible. A lot of it was over our heads, which was why we needed others with credentials and degrees to interpret it for us (she strongly recommended the clergy of the mainstream Protestant church where she was a proud member and chairwoman of the sanctuary decorating committee). According to Helga, although God had spoken to people eons ago, after the last sentence in Revelations was penned, He'd clammed up for the rest of time.

I could not comprehend what she was saying, and started to feel less like an idiot and more like someone from another planet. How could the realities of two people who both believed in the same God differ so drastically? If, as she said, God's work with man was finished, where had He gone and what was He doing? And why *couldn't* I understand the Bible myself? I'd been reading it every day and wasn't having any problems so far.

Helga's tight-lipped summation was geared to shut me up for good: she hoped I would give serious thought to how ridiculous, sacrilegious, arrogant and insane I sounded before I went around claiming that I was having conversations with God. Convinced she'd cured me, she spun on her heel and left me to consider the benefits of more conventional religious pursuits that didn't involve straying from the herd.

I sorely regretted ever having opened my mouth. I was much younger than Helga, respected her, and had no rebuttal for her harsh reprieve. She'd cut me off at the knees, and for a long time after that I secretly struggled with whether or not she could be right. I certainly *was* nobody, so why *would* God talk to me?

But something else inside my heart (the Holy Spirit!) argued with her words. If it wasn't God's voice I'd heard, whose *was* it? The dialogue had taken place while I was in prayer, and the things I'd been told were far above my own thinking. I supposed it was possible that I was delusional, but I'd never been accused of that before. I was living an average life and in the course of it I was encountering other average folks who had conversations with God, too. They weren't raging fanatics, nor did any of them think they were special. They had simply invited Him into their hearts and lives. It was also my observation that we were by and large a whole lot happier than Helga.

As it turned out, accepting Helga's judgment would have closed the door on a life that has been spiritually rich and overflowing with the joy of discovery.

As years passed, I continued to talk to God and learned to recognize the Voice that answered me. Our Father's words are consistently loving, strong, comforting, uplifting and wise beyond human thought. Any voice that degrades, discourages, wounds, or tears down with guilt or condemnation, is *not* His. God's correction, when we are in need of it, is honest, direct, and permeated with mercy and unconditional love. His warnings are those of a loving Father Who does not desire to see His children deceived, but wants to enlighten and empower them instead. Our humbled souls feel and know the difference.

Our Creator's words can be revolutionary and are often at odds with human reasoning, which is no doubt why Jesus' disciples often had a difficult time with some of the things He said. *"Master, this is too hard for us to understand!"* • John 6:60   We can be assured that even when we don't grasp what He's saying at the time, the lesson will be demonstrated through circumstances further down the road. • I Corinthians 1:18-25

The Word of God is described as *"...quick and powerful and sharper than any two edged sword, piercing even to the dividing asunder of soul and spirit...and is a discerner of the thoughts and intents of the heart."* • Hebrews 4:12

Jesus is the Prince of Peace, but He also said He had *"...come to bring the sword."* When the Holy Spirit speaks, the words cleave to our deepest heart and accomplish what God sent them to do. We may find ourselves beautifully broken, and we may bleed, but in the next instant, the process of healing and restoration begins, and He fills us with peace and joy. • Matthew 10:34

The words God speaks to us today will never contradict what He spoke to those before us. *"I am the Lord, I change not."* • Malachi 3:6 At their core, the messages are always the same, and we will consistently find parallels and confirmations within the scriptures.

Helga was right about one thing: God has indeed already said it all throughout the ages. But since she didn't have regular conversations with Him, she didn't know that He is faithful to repeat Himself constantly in fresh ways that cast light on His truths and principles from different angles. This is so that those who may have difficulty grasping them in one way will be able to see and understand them in another. Hebrew, Greek, the language of King James or modern English – it's the heart of the message that is sacred. And that's why He keeps speaking – hoping we will listen, and talk with Him.

I've never forgotten my exchange with Helga, and though I could not have imagined it then, I am thankful, now, for that coarse thread to weave into this message.

For as long as I knew her she nurtured bitterness, resentment and envy, refused to unwind, and was never genuinely happy. Ultimately, in the words of someone who saw her awhile back, she "turned to stone." I tried in countless ways over the years to share with her the freedom and love I had found, but Helga's God lives in a box and anything outside of that box is suspicious, dangerous or frivolous. Her religion is a social exercise that requires unquestioning service and the adapting of one's ethical, moral, and political beliefs to whatever position the present ruling council has voted to adopt.

I feel sad for those who believe that the One to whom they pray is so remote and detached that He would never reach down to embrace them or help them up when they fall. They call Him "Father," but would not dream of running to His arms or asking Him to heal their broken hearts or dreams. They think He never leaves His throne and has already done everything He's going to do – that He's an ancient, impersonal Deity with no desire for personal contact with His creations. They cannot conceive that He would want to hold them on His lap, teach them, protect them, whisper secrets to them, hug them, laugh with them or dry their tears.

Somewhere, sometime, in a solemn, secret chamber, a starchy holy council probably hammered out the criteria that must be met for an individual to hear God. I'll bet a curriculum even exists. But what about those of us who can't afford the tuition? Do some get to hear and others not?

Dear Helga, you are God's child! We are **all** His children! What loving Father doesn't talk to His children?

64

There are messages and prophecies to be found within this book. They have been included only after much prayer, soul-searching, and the passage of time, until I received the assurance that the words were meant to be shared.

If a passage seems to have been written just for you, it was. When God speaks, His words are a golden key that unlocks our secret heart.

ॐ

S.G.Rose

66

The Rose

~ I ~

$\mathscr{L}$ife was as perfect as I'd ever dreamed it could be on that warm, October afternoon. We lived in a cozy hand-hewn house then, tucked into a little clearing in the forest, hidden safely away from the rest of the world. When winter snows blanketed the roof, apple cider and hearty stew simmered in kettles atop the wood stove, and the smell of freshly baked bread wafted through our homemade heaven. In springtime, the children and I caught polliwogs, gathered trilliums and hunted for mushrooms beneath the towering cottonwoods. Summer's highlight was the old-fashioned small town Fourth of July celebration, with pony rides, patchwork quilts spread out under ancient oak trees, picnic baskets filled with fried chicken and raspberry scones – and the magic of fireworks beneath the stars.

$\mathscr{A}$utumn's spell was the sweetest of them all. It's always been my favorite season. I was born then – perhaps that is why. Autumn turned our forest red and yellow, crisp and pungent like the apples in the old orchard at the end of the road. In the shadow of Mt. Rainier, the changing leaves were breathtaking. Magenta, gold, crimson and every shade in between, they stole the stage from all of nature as they danced to earth for their final bow. A sign, perhaps, that some things are their most beautiful at the time of passing.

$\mathscr{B}$ut on that flawless day, I wasn't pondering my mortality. I was thirty years old, in love with life and my young family, and bursting with dreams and plans. It was time for lunch, so I called my two little boys in from their play. After they'd finished eating, I put them down for their naps and headed back through the house to the laundry room. On the way, I glanced out the front window, and a spot of color near the garden caught my eye. Guessing it was a toy that needed to be retrieved, I detoured to the front door, happy for the excuse to go outside. Laundry could wait – the autumn sun might not.

I stepped off the porch onto the path that led to our little garden plot and the gravel crunched beneath my feet. Our hopes had been high when we planted the seeds for our favorite vegetables, but three months later it was safe to say that none of our scrawny produce would be sporting ribbons at the county fair. Only a few brave peas, zucchini and cucumbers had managed to sprout in the hard, rocky soil, and ever since they'd shown their heads, the onslaught of voracious slugs, deer, and other unseen critters had been shocking. I didn't like fighting nature, and had decided I would be content with gathering wild edibles thereafter.

Our new puppy trotted faithfully in my shadow and the soft music of the forest played around me. I loved it so! My heart sang with joy and I breathed my thanks to God. I wanted nothing more than to live there in that humble little homestead forever.

*T*he year before, we'd inherited a few shrubs and bushes from the yard of a home that was being excavated for an addition. Among them was a weather-beaten old rose bush which I imagined must have been glorious in its day. I'd had a special love of roses since childhood, so was saddened to see this valiant old bush damaged beyond saving. Its roots had been sheared off by the blade of the shovel, and it was split down the middle at its base. The bleached, brittle wood made me suspect that it had been dead long before it was dug from the ground. Regrettably, we'd tossed it in the direction of the burn pile beyond the garden, where it was soon swallowed by weeds and where it had lain, forgotten, ever since.

I shielded my eyes from the bright sun as I neared the spot of color that had drawn me outside, and could not believe what I saw. There, rising from a clump of tall grass, was one solitary slender stem crowned by a perfect pink rose.

It wasn't possible for that old rose bush to be alive! Incredulously, I reached out, touched the bloom, and bent to inhale its delicate fragrance. As I looked at it in awe, sacred energy filled the air. God's presence surrounded me and I knew He had called me outside for a reason. I opened my heart and listened.

"My daughter, you are this rose. In your life there will be hardship and pain. You will be wounded, rejected and cast aside. For a time you may feel your life is over, but you will only be resting. I will

protect you, sustain you and keep you from destruction. Endure bravely all that is to come and wait for My time. In the autumn of your life you will bloom again, just as this rose – a bloom as beautiful as those of your youth, but stronger because you will have prevailed against all odds. This symbol of triumph and love will be a testimony of encouragement to others. Mark my promise upon your heart now while it is warm with joy, and when winter comes, your soul shall find comfort. You are My autumn rose."

How, when everything was so wonderful and the future so bright, could I comprehend what had just been spoken to me? It was impossible to imagine how any of the human emotions that I would equate with that battered old rose bush could enter my happy life. But the sense of holiness and the love within the message were undeniable. I couldn't understand it, and I hoped I had heard wrong, but the instant I entertained that possibility, my Father removed any questions in my mind about what He'd said.

I lingered there for long moments, touching the petals of the brave bloom before me. Finally, I went back inside, got my camera and took a picture of the rose. Then, I locked God's words in my heart and promised Him that I would not forget.

~ *II* ~

By the time I'd reached the age of forty, much of the autumn rose prophecy had come to pass in my life. Although God's promise did not lessen my human pain, I always knew how much He loved me and that one day, joy would return again. The comfort and hope He'd told me to hide in my heart had protected me from what would otherwise have been destruction and despair.

I didn't know exactly what God considered "autumn" to be in human years, but whenever it was, I longed for it arrive quickly. In the meantime, He seemed to be in no hurry to get me there. Through one trial after another, He supernaturally renewed my strength and even kept me looking and feeling much younger than my years. I could never account for that, and when people accused me of lying about my age (presumably they thought I should look much worse for the wear), I would tell them I had claimed two powerful Scripture passages as my own: Psalms 103 and Isaiah 40:31.

"Bless the Lord, O my soul: and all that is within me, bless His holy Name...
and forget not all His benefits...Who forgives all your iniquities,
Who heals all your diseases, Who redeems your life from destruction,
Who crowns you with loving kindness and tender mercies,
Who satisfies your mouth with good things,
so that your youth is renewed like the eagle's..."

Psalm 103:1-5

"But those who wait on the Lord shall renew their strength;
they shall mount up with wings like eagles,
they shall run and not be weary,
they shall walk and not faint."

Isaiah 40:31

Every time I remembered the rose of my youth, my faith would be renewed and I would be enabled to press on, for I knew God's best was yet to come. The assurance of His constant loving care was my saving grace, but I knew that there were multitudes of hurting women who did not have that comfort. My heart ached for them to know how precious they were to their Heavenly Father, and that they could trust His perfect plan. I wrote this poem for my sisters.

The rose spoke to me in the garden, one day,

words so gentle, 'twas an angel, I thought.
I could not have imagined the thing she would say,
nor its comfort could fortune have bought.

Skies were grey when I'd pruned back the dead

of her wandering stems, grown wild,
"Life will return in the spring," I had said,
as upon the hot fire they piled.

Her barren existence seemed much like my own,

through dark years I thought never would end,

70

and rigid in silence, she stood there alone,
her thorns no delight to her friend.

I had almost forgotten her glory in bloom

when sprang forth brave new shoots, spite the cold!
And my spirit rejoiced, for I knew that soon,
her blossoms again would unfold.

*T*hen that sudden warm day

came with hope's fervent blush,
and I looked out my window to see
a burst of bright color upon that old bush ~
a messenger calling to me!

I ran to the yard, cupped her face in my hand,

stroked her petals upon my pale cheek,
her fragrance was flawless,
to breathe it, so grand,
then my awed human heart heard her speak.

"Dearest, you fear life has lost goodness, all,

doubt that joy can return to your soul.
the thorns that adorn you seem never to fall,
while your petals have dropped long ago.

Precious flowers you offered so freely in love

others plucked and then left you to die
I'm to tell you this all has been seen from Above,
and that you are just like I.

For there is One who has tended your life

though the weather was stormy and cold
He's labored beside you through struggle and strife
and cared for you, young until old.

You are His project, His treasure, His prize,

every scar, every bloom bears His name.
His patience is perfect, His plan ever wise

and throughout all your years 'twill remain.
He charts the seasons, the changes they bring,
and His hand shapes your life if you trust.
In mercy, He prunes when your heart cannot sing,
to bring forth greater beauty, He must.

Sister, with such joy you do touch me now,
that winter's harsh woes are erased,
and lavish sweet praises upon my fresh brow
for the new life these coarse sticks encased.

So forget not the promise I share in this place,
clasp it tightly upon thy breast,
for the moment shall come
when Love's breath strokes your face,
to this, with my life I attest!

Endure every winter, but forsake not spring's dream,
Life returns, my brave lady! And then,
our Master will smile and whisper sweet,
*You shall **always** bloom again!*

~ III ~

*A*s more years passed, and I found myself uprooted time and time again, I learned a great elemental truth: I could not allow physical surroundings or circumstances to dictate my happiness.

I was a diehard nester, and forever longing for *Home, Sweet Home,* where I could settle in and live happily ever after. God, on the other hand, wanted me to learn how to be content *wherever* He had put me. Furthermore, while I was longing for "someday," I was missing the beauty of the present (which was the someday I had been waiting for earlier).

On the day that this revelation finally sank in, my life changed. Here on this planet I am a pilgrim, a pioneer. Whether God houses me in a mansion or a travel trailer makes no difference. It is all the same: *temporary*. My true home is with Him. *He* is my dwelling place, now and forever.

I run to be with You

here at this desk, my sanctuary.
Moving boxes surround me again, always so much unknown,
mother and children alone,
Oh, how we need You, Father.

I wait for Your touch, Your voice ~ for the words

that will drop like honey on my hungry, trembling heart.
Only You sustain me.

The sound of this old, familiar typewriter is my music

as Your love songs dance from my fingertips in the night.
The golden melody of Your truth kisses my soul,
I hide in You, my home.

Sweet and holy is this service I do ~ and not service at all,

Bliss.
Paradise is this time spent with You,
where daydreams become sublime.

Too many years of my life have passed

here in this unfriendly place.
To cheer my heart, You planted roses before I came.

The front door is open a crack,

one bloom on a bush in view ~ pink, like one so long ago
when I was as innocent as its blush.

Sudden sunlight streams in, I hear Your voice,

"The Sign...My message...
do you remember them, My child?"

Yes, Father! I remember!
I am willing to begin again ~ and again,
there is no other plan.
My branches are less heavy with stubborn thorns these days,
and I shall wait to unfold, one petal at a time,
by Your design not mine.

Fragrance, texture unchanging,

Seasons long passing.
I have never stopped believing Your promise
and I shall bloom

For You.

~ IV ~

As I write these lines, I am in my 50th year. Another child of autumn, my first granddaughter, has just been born. As her tiny fingers curl around mine, my thoughts travel back to her father's chubby little fists clasping the bouquet of dandelions he'd picked for me from the yard. That cherished moment, and another of his brother hugging our puppy, live in frames on my dresser, alongside a faded old photograph of a pink rose blooming beside a burn pile.

On the weekend of my birthday, I drove out to the country to the acres where our little house stood. The alder grove that supplied our firewood had reseeded itself and grown so thick and tall that the house was no longer visible from the road. I didn't venture down the long, winding driveway – a *No Trespassing* sign hung from a rusty chain across the entrance.

In my memory, everything is perfect there. Smoke curls from the chimney and the pumpkins sit on the porch waiting for their faces. A roly-poly toddler and a giggling four-year-old play on the tire swing while a furry little dog races around chasing squirrels up the trees. The

74

forest fills my senses. I can smell the ferns, feel the coarse bark of the freshly-split alder, taste the tart red huckleberries. Those were the happiest days of my life...and because of God's grace, so are these. But I will always ache to go back. To push the swing, hug my babies, play with the dog, stack the firewood, make a pie...pick the rose and bring it inside. I never did, you know. I just let it bloom.

S.G.Rose

S.G.Rose

76

Runner

C reated in Your image I run this race:
The Marathon of Humanness.

G olden thread shimmers at my feet
leading me on,
weaving its way through my consciousness...
hidden too often
in the dust and mud of this well worn track.

Q uestions chart my course...
I run leaving everything behind,
Earth time's final stretch in sight.

I sprinted my youth with my chin held high,
leapt hurdles with ease.
Eyes fixed on the prize,
I never saw the threatening sky
'til lightning struck my unguarded heart
and took me down mid stride.

S tronger runners passed me by,
winning the cheers of the crowd.
Bruised and stunned,
I heard my Coach yell:
"Get up! This isn't over yet!"
I obeyed His command,
and lap after lap
the pounding of my heart and feet
were all I could hear.

I pace myself now,
imperfections accepted,
failures forgiven.

D id my soul train for this somewhere
before the challenge began?
Did I come here prepared?
How much did I bring?
How much have I learned?
How much did I choose?
How much can I endure?

I s it really about me at all?
What I feel,
Whether I win,
What I think I need,
How much I bleed?

C reated in Your image,
Runner crowned with thorns…
given this chance to shine for those whose champion I am,
and to leave them with the memory
of a race they saw well run.

≈

Hebrews 12:1-2

2 Timothy 4:7-8

The Pebble

For many weeks I'd been praying desperately for doors to open in my life. (Everywhere I looked, God's work was waiting to be done, and I was convinced that if I saw a need, I was the one meant to meet it. I hadn't yet come to the awareness that God might not be in such a hurry as I, or that the planet would keep turning with or without my tireless efforts.) Though I meant well, my desires always seemed to race ahead of my ability to make them reality. This had resulted in an underlying, nagging feeling that I was never doing quite enough.

(When my anxious petitions to God were continually met with silence, my frustration grew. I wanted a brilliant flash of insight or a sign, but neither came. No answers. No miraculous intervention to catapult me forward through open doors. I regularly prayed with others who were seeking direction, and they received it, so where was *mine*? I felt helpless, stuck, thwarted. My plans were not progressing and my goals were no closer. I feared that what I longed to achieve would never happen.)

My melancholy had no doubt been amplified by the long, dreary Northwest winter, but spring had finally arrived, and on one rare, warm day, I was drawn outside to a park near the ocean. The grounds were deserted, and after walking for awhile, I sat down on a patch of grass next to a stream, and surrendered to the peace of the idyllic setting. The sun and blue skies lifted my heart, the smells of spring were sweet, and the crisp breeze cleared some of the clutter from my mind. I hoped, as always, to hear God, but wasn't going to allow myself any expectations.

I watched the stream and envied its freedom, freshness and natural, easy purpose as it meandered through the woodland pasture on its way to the saltwater not far beyond. Oh, for life to be that easy.

After about twenty minutes of solitude, my heart heard the gentle words, *"Pick up a pebble and toss it into the brook."*

I wanted to believe the directive was from the Holy Spirit, but logic argued that such an act would be natural for anyone sitting beside a stream. I disregarded the inner voice and kept my arms wrapped around my knees.

"Pick up a pebble and toss it into the brook!" The urging was more insistent the second time.

Well, what difference would it make if I did? I picked up a little stone and I replied under my breath to myself, *"Okay, I'm doing it, but I already know this lesson. It will make a small splash in the water and then send out rings...etc., etc., etc."* I had really been hoping for a new revelation, but I tossed the stone anyway.

Plunk. My aim was poor. The pebble bounced off a bigger rock and slid down into a little pool at the edge of the stream without creating even the smallest ripple. I laughed at myself for being such a die-hard for spiritual signs as to keep looking for them when it was obvious they weren't going to come. If I was to find some meaning in this exercise, it was only that I felt just like that pebble. It plunked and then sank, unnoticed, while the cheery stream tumbled by. I stared at the water some more and felt depressed.

Then, a strong urge drew me to look more closely at the little pool at the edge of the brook. As I bent over and peered down into it, the loving voice of my Heavenly Father filled my mind.

"My child, when you learn to yield to silence and to practice patience, you will not demand immediate results. I am creating a new life within you which must be incubated in quietness, not in the cold, rapidly-moving mainstream where it would be swept away by a torrent of activity. It could not survive there. Look even closer at the little pool where the pebble fell. It is not unimportant, stagnant or without purpose as you may think. I am the rock, you are the pebble and the pool is a birthplace."

I gazed deeper, past the reflection of my own face. Away from the strong current, fed only by a gentle trickle, the pool rested serenely. Because it was still, the sun had been able to penetrate its depths and I saw that it was filled with new life. Tiny snails clung to clumps of moss, and fingerlings scurried under the silt at the bottom when I touched the surface. How fragile and precious these small creatures were, sheltered there in that seemingly insignificant puddle!

Comfort, joy and understanding flooded into my heart. I saw that I had muddied God's plans with my restless, endless stirring. I had never waited long enough for things to settle and clear so that I could see the larger picture, and my clouded perception had obscured the joys of small beginnings.

80

Many of us have yearned passionately to be one with the flowing water – to jump in, make a splash and see action – to be a mighty channel of power and blessing, or at least a lovely brook. If our Creator has separated us out from all of that, it's for a vital purpose – He's nurturing new life.

Silent times are not punishments, they are protected sanctuaries. If we allow ourselves to rest there, deeper understanding, higher perspective and greater strength will be born. Though growth is imperceptible to the human eye, it is happening, nevertheless.

When we learn to recognize these incubation times as part of the Divine process, we will welcome them and submit to them patiently – whether we detect progress or not. The profound is hidden within the simple. From the silence we will emerge changed and ready to reenter the flow, prepared for what God sees downstream.

Answers come in quietness, seldom in the noise of many waters. To hear them we must learn to be still.

I am no longer impatient with efforts that remain small. Puddles are okay. Life is very peaceful there. Raging rivers and thundering rapids? Not unless He tells me I have to go.

૭

"Be still and know that I am God." • Psalm 46:10

S.G.Rose

82

When

When I was young, Time took too long,
dreams danced before me to tunes yet sung.
I rushed headstrong toward every dream,
impatient roads stretched far.
I had to taste, to explore, to prove
I could carve my worth
on this Earth
Then.

I touched every star I'd climbed to find,
some sparkled, some burned,
some fell and died...
some were illusions of my mind.
Time picked up pace somewhere
but I wasn't watching the sands in the hourglass
as the days trickled down.
Expectations spurred me on –
so sure I'd be happy
When.

Calendar pages turned faster each year,
tides changed,
swept me to distant unknown shores
where I learned to abide,
yet I hungered still – unsatisfied.

Time, my Enemy,

Time, my Friend...

(I know now what I didn't know then.
Life unfolds one petal at a time.
Restless creature, willful child...
I thought the control was mine.)

We come here on a scavenger hunt,
jump into the game to win...
search for things of no value,
hold them for only an instant,
before they belong to

Then.

Storm ~ be silent!

Mind ~ be still!

Heart ~ listen to yourself beating!

(The moment to cherish

is Now.)

❧

84

Questions

If my poems become my prayers,
and my prayers turn into poems...
when my mind wanders off onto side-tracks of contemplation,
and I ask You a million questions before You can answer the first...
is that okay with You
?

When moments in Your presence turn into hours of dreaming...
and what should be hours of prayer lasts only moments...
do You wish I were more consistent
?

When I promise You I will...and then I don't,
and I vow that I won't...but then I do,
I'm so disappointed in myself.
Did You already know
?

Do I try too hard, or not hard enough?
Have I drug my feet, or run too fast?
Shall I ever know what might have been?
Was there an alternate plan?
Or does the perfect one unfold before me each passing day
as I skip and stumble along behind You
?

I suppose the rest doesn't really matter so much ~ does it, Lord
?

Romans 7:15-25; 8:1-2

85

THE TREE

"Blessed is the man that trusts in the Lord and whose hope the Lord is.
For he shall be as a tree planted by the waters,
that spreads out its roots by the river,
That does not see when heat comes, but its leaf shall be green;
and shall not be full of cares in the years of drought,
neither shall cease from yielding fruit. "

Jeremiah 17:7-8

Evening had marked the merciful end to another difficult, frustrating and exhausting day. Like an endless string of rusty boxcars loaded with adversity, they'd been careening noisily through my life for weeks on end, and there was no caboose in sight.

I felt like a soldier with a sword permanently welded to my hand – a warrior who appeared strong and valiant, but who was, in reality, drained, discouraged, and lacked the strength to head out to the front lines again the next morning. Would the battles ever end? Somewhere I'd gotten the impression that spiritual awareness was going to make things easier, but it seemed like the opposite was happening. Was this what I should expect from now on? One problem after another? Surely I must be doing something wrong!

I sat down, rested my weary head in my hands, and prepared to discuss the latest mess with God, Who I desperately hoped had answers.

He didn't send a balloon bouquet to my pity party, or dispel my troubles with the wave of a magic wand, but His message was a permanent fix for my recurring confusion: *Enlightenment.*

I closed my eyes, but before I could form the first word of my prayer, all of my attention was commanded by a dramatic living picture that had been projected into my mind.

A magnificent, mystical tree of massive proportions dominated the scene before me. Light seemed to emanate from within it, causing every detail of the thick, dense branches and lush, vibrant green canopy to stand out vividly against the deep twilight sky.

Enormous, shimmering fruits of an indescribable luminous silver-gold color hung in profusion from the limbs. They were ripened to perfection and I was overwhelmed by the desire to pick one, for I knew instinctively that it would burst with sweetness and nourishment.

In bold contrast to the loveliness of the succulent fruits, the massive trunk was coarse and scarred from many years of pruning and storms. I looked closer and saw the initials of those who had taken refuge beneath its boughs carved into its side. It was solid, powerful, unmovable – a symbol of tremendous endurance and strength, and a place of shelter and safety, peace and rest.

As I marveled at its grandeur, the awareness formed that I was being shown *The Tree of Life*.

The potential for tremendous beauty, strength and abundant fruit lies within each of us "planted" here by the Lord – for the purpose that we might be a blessing to others. God was showing me, from *His* point of view, what I – a scraggly little sapling struggling for survival – could become. Our Creator looks gently upon us with patient, eternal eyes, and He had more to show me about the process of growth.

The picture changed and the ground became transparent, allowing me to see into the depths of the earth beneath the tree. My initial reaction was aversion to what appeared to be a dark underworld where a colossal battle for survival raged. Unlovely in every respect, it was the direct opposite of the glory and beauty of the upper tree.

Countless tangled roots engaged in a monumental struggle as they fought their way downward. Stones, clay, and boulders blocked their paths and threatened to impede their progress, but the roots had relentlessly pressed on, for to have stopped at these obstacles would have meant the end of their growth.

Then, God drew my eyes to the different ways in which the roots had prevailed against the hardships, and I realized that the scene was not a brutal battle, but a passionate quest for life.

Some of the roots had forced their way between the rocks and pushed them aside. Others had pressed against layers of hardened clay until they had ultimately broken through. And many had embraced the boulders that stood in their way, turning the obstructions into anchors. In this complex, awe-inspiring picture of profound patience and endurance, the most obvious, dominant factor was this: *the size and fruitfulness of the upper tree was the direct result of what was happening below.*

One scripture calls us *"...the planting of the Lord."* As we begin to grow and send down roots, we will inevitably encounter difficulties and roadblocks that may seem impossible – or at least aggravating and exhausting – to overcome. We will repeatedly be faced with opposition to our spiritual and emotional growth, and must choose to press on or stay where we are. If we do the latter, there may be an initial feeling of relief, but what will follow it? If we stop reaching deeper, our growth will be stunted and part of us will shrink and die. If we give up the fight, "the rock and the hard place" will have won. Without strong, healthy roots, the upper tree will not grow larger or bear more fruit, and may not survive the next storm. Shallow roots – even hundreds of them spreading out in all directions – will not anchor a tree in hurricane force winds. *Depth* is what we need.

The only way we can truly identify one another's character is by the visible fruits we bear. *"By their fruits you will know them."* • Jesus, Matthew 7:16-20 Most of us want to bear good fruit, but it's easy to forget that this depends solely upon the victories within our roots. If we have per-severed, prevailed and grown, we will naturally produce the fruits of the Spirit. They will be visible to others, and those who are weary, hungry, and thirsty will find rest, shelter, and nourishment for their souls. They will be fed, encouraged, and restored, for the life within the fruit will have been drawn up from the deep wellspring of the Holy Spirit.

God never said spiritual growth would be comfortable or easy, and that fact should actually bring us tremendous relief. Our thirst cannot be satisfied unless we allow each new challenge to continually push us further and deeper into the Spirit. The closer we are to God, the more nourishment we will receive, which encourages more roots to sprout...and then the cycle repeats. This all happens so slowly that we do not perceive it. Little wonder that we feel impatient and lost at times!

We should not be surprised or discouraged that this journey of our roots commands the focus of our attention. *The miracle is that while we are concentrating on survival, the upper tree is simultaneously manifesting a life of its own.* If total objectivity was possible, and we could dig up from the dirt into the daylight and perceive ourselves through the eyes of others, we might be very surprised at the beauty and strength they see.

T rees – and souls – take time to grow. The fruits of the Spirit cannot be forced. They are conceived by, born of and belong to our Creator, as do we – *"The planting of the Lord,"* who bear them. Seasons, pruning, storms and harvests are all within His Divine control. Our only task is to continue to send down roots – right where we're planted.

"The fruit of the Spirit is love, joy, peace, patience, kindness, goodness, faithfulness, gentleness and self control..."
•
Galatians 5:22-23

"...That they might be called trees of righteousness, the planting of the Lord..."
•
Isaiah 61:3

"Herein is my Father glorified, that you bear much fruit; so shall you be my disciples."
•
Jesus ~ John 15:8

Seasons

I was born in early spring

at the dawn of life's promised best...
securely held in the love and light
that bathed my Mother's breast.

The seed of Truth had taken root,

my cramped prison I'd left below...
and I stretched upward to meet the sun,
so fearless and eager to grow.

Deep breaths I took of the Spirit's wind,

its power and strength filled my soul...
rain from Above soaked into my heart,
and thus nurtured, I was whole.

My songs soon rang throughout the land,

I sang them to all who came near...
told of the darkness I'd conquered brave,
and my new life planted here.

They marveled, then,

and admired my strength,
loved my blossoms' fragrance, sweet...
came to be near me, brought others along
to sit there at my feet.

Embraced by warmth, I grew lush and full,

the kind Gardener shared my days...
the fruit I bore, I offered to Him
in thanks for His tender ways.

Standing tall was easy then,

for my purpose was clearly seen…
Heaven's favor poured down and I was blessed,
abundant and ever increasing.

✸

I thought it strange when the colors changed,

and pondered the reason why…
the greens turned yellow, brown and red
and the blue faded in the sky.

Mysterious mists arrived in the night

and shrouded me past the dawn…
I waited for the Gardener – when would He come?
Where were the birds with their song?

Shadows crept into my afternoons,

the air had a bite I'd not known…
my hill grew quiet, no visitors came,
I didn't like being alone.

I shivered and tried to ignore the chill,

prayed the sun would shine…
reminded myself of all I possessed,
and that everything would be fine.

A few withered fruits hung from naked limbs,

they were all that now remained…
the leaves had fallen from my once lush boughs
and my pride had turned to shame.

Seeing me thus, the Gardener came

walking slowly toward my hill...
with great relief I awaited Him there,
surely He'd help, He'd heal!

I noticed the shears He held in His hand,

but they couldn't be for me...
perhaps for the berry vines growing wild...
I was His *special* tree.

Well, a small snip or two of a twig, I could bear,

if He said it should be so...
I'd seen Him tend others that way at times
though why, I did not know.

When He arrived, He set quickly to work,

and in shocked disbelief I looked down...
as severed swift, each cherished branch
fell crashing to the ground.

He bent and tossed them all aside

as if they had no worth...
yet my greatest triumphs were lying there dead
upon the lap of earth.

The match was set, the flames leapt high,

I saw in the smoke, my doom...
my hopes and dreams turned slowly to ash,
upon the blaze consumed.

Why me? What purpose could there be

for me to suffer so...
when the Gardener's hands were the very ones
that had always helped me grow!

"What did I do wrong!?" I cried aloud,

"Can't You see the pain I'm in?
Nothing You say can replace what I've lost...
I'll never grow again!

What of our partnership, Yours and mine,

I thought we were a team!
You blessed and I bore, I gave You my all!
What foretold this cruel scene?

I placed all of my trust in You –

why, 'twas not so long ago
You picked and praised the fruits I bore,
and now You wound me so!

You stand looking on as this fire burns,

my reward is this bitter end?
Never again can I lift my head
nor shall I call You, 'friend!'"

He listened patiently, waited to speak,

I tried to read His face...
I wanted the sympathy I deserved,
but could not find a trace.

I wept in anger, refused to hear...

His soft words met defiance.
Until finally, He gathered His tools
and walked sadly away in silence.

❄

In the empty months that followed that day,

 I retreated deep within...
poor in spirit, out of tune
with Creator's earth, and Him.

There seemed no promise of life again

for what little of me there remained...
every bitter storm left another mark
and I looked for someone to blame.

Those few who passed by were unimpressed,

 if they noticed me at all...
they lent me no hope and I heard them discuss
how even the chosen can fall.

Abandoned there, I submitted to fate...

 to stand was the most I could do...
in this frigid world where no flowers bloomed
and my tears had replaced the dew.

I mourned the loss of my cradle, warm,

 taken for granted before...
my only peace now was to slumber beneath
the cold blanket of snow I wore.

For sleep brought escape, and the hope of dreams

 filled with treasured memories
of robins, the laughter of children at play,
and whispers in my leaves.

Father Time limped by and moaned his tune,

 "Your past is gone, let it die..."
but I couldn't let go of the days I'd known
when Love stood by my side.

❖

Early one morning, I woke to a sound,

whether by chance or by will...
and saw someone approaching – a man I knew –
'twas the Gardener upon my hill!

As He came close, I thrilled at the sight...

I'd forgotten how long it had been
since I had seen that familiar face,
yet there'd been no change in Him.

I had no words, and neither did He

as He reached out His callused hand...
to stroke my cold arms, brush the moss away,
while I sought to understand.

Why had He returned? I deserved it not.

Humbled, I hung my head...
I could not hide my barrenness,
and feared He'd think me dead.

Then something moved through me at His touch...

a longing I could not deny...
to serve Him again however I could,
and I began to cry.

Compassion filled those holy eyes,

as they searched my scars, my face...
then suddenly I saw Him smile
and from that smile flowed grace.

A stirring began somewhere deep inside

the heart I'd thought was stone…
something awakening…could it be?
Yes! *Blossoms* in my bones!

How small and selfish my thoughts had been,

as though I were the only one…
wrapped up in my sorrow I had not seen
that in wisdom each season must come.

I'd mistaken my pruning for loss, not gain,

had cursed the winter's test…
I'd closed my eyes to the higher plan,
while the Gardener had seen the rest.

The fruit yet to come would feed many more

for the passing of this time…
He'd always known I would bear it again,
but the reasons could not be mine.

*"To everything there is a season,
and a time to every purpose under Heaven…"*
•
Ecclesiastes 3:1-11

*"I am the true vine and my Father is the Gardener…every branch in me that
bears fruit, He prunes so that it may bring forth more fruit.
I am the vine, you are the branches. He that abides in me and I in him bears
much fruit…In this is my Father glorified."*
•
Jesus, John 15:1-8

97

S.G.Rose

GUARDED
HEART

Guarded heart
You are so alone
Behind walls of fear
Built stone upon stone.

Can hope reach through
Its light warm your skin
Aren't you cold
Hiding there within?

Emotions brought pain
So you've locked them away
Think you'll take them out only
On some perfect day.

If you let nothing touch you
◆ Desensitized ◆

I pray that Love
Takes you quite by surprise.

✦

I John 4:7-11

S.G.Rose

100

Blessed

Blessed are those who believe Love heals
And embrace its cleansing tide,
Who shed their pain and begin again,
Who leave behind fear and pride.

Blessed are those whose eyes look with grace
Upon all that has been and will be,
With gentle acceptance of the lessons learned
On the way to becoming free.

Blessed are those who make soft the place
Where seeds of change can grow,
Let life's pages unfold through seasons held dear,
Cherished, and then, let go.

Blessed are those brave soldiers who tell
Of this battle and bear its scars,
Who laid down their weapons, in forgiveness found peace,
Who broke through self's prison bars.

Blessed are we when this long journey leads
To a place of higher sight,
When the crooked path lies behind and below
And ahead, shine lands of light.

Blessed are you for calling me Friend,
For the times you've been my guide,
For sharing your love with this wandering heart,
For walking awhile by my side.

Blessed am I that God loves me so
To complete this tapestry,
To answer the prayers I was too weak to pray
And unravel the mystery of me.

᠊ꙮ᠊

S.G.Rose

The Storm

*F*air winds and a cloudless sky promised a pleasant passage for the thirteen men preparing to cast off from shore late that day. One of them, a fisherman named Peter, had proposed they sail across the Sea of Galilee, and when the others agreed, he'd stowed his nets and gear in record time. Now, he was itching to be underway before anyone changed their mind.

Crowds made Peter uncomfortable, and he'd spent the past several days being jostled by throngs of people who'd been following them from village to village along the coast. The salt air and open water had been calling to him, and a quiet cruise at the helm of his skiff would be a blessed escape

The pragmatic fisherman knew he should try to be more tolerant, but dealing with the public demanded more refined social skills than he possessed. He longed for the early days when he'd first met Yeshua, and their small group had formed. None of them could have imagined, back then, how drastically their rather ordinary lives would change, or that privacy and anonymity would become rare commodities.

*T*hey lived in tumultuous times. Change was coming, and their leader was at the heart of it. Peter was a down-to-earth man, and although he felt humbled and privileged to have been chosen to join Yeshua on the leading edge of a spiritual revolution, there were occasions on which it overwhelmed him. He hoped that they would arrive unnoticed at their destination so that they could enjoy at least one peaceful night before word got out that they were in the area.

Yeshua was tired but happy when he climbed aboard, and appeared thankful for the time away with his friends. Although he was their leader, they were beginning to feel more protective of him all the time. Wherever he went, he was mobbed by people with problems, and he never turned anyone away. His teachings had made him a controversial figure, and along with his fans, his enemies also showed up regularly these days, hurling insults and shouting threats. His endurance and unfailing compassion were impressive, but his disciples wondered if

103

he knew his own limits. Tonight, they hoped to see him get some well-deserved rest.

Peter's practiced hand rested easy on the tiller while he mentally calculated the crossing time. He'd fished these waters all his life and knew them well. With this perfect breeze, the trip wouldn't take long, and there might even be time to drop the nets for awhile offshore before they headed in. He leaned back, stretched out his legs, and sighed with contentment as he scanned the horizon. The silhouetted sails of a few smaller boats stood out against the first streaks of sunset color, but they were keeping a respectful distance.

The boat glided effortlessly through the water, and the sound of the waves splashing softly against the hull soon washed away all stress. The men's day had begun before dawn, and they were exhausted. Rocked by the sea, they relaxed and lapsed into companionable silence.

Peter caught Yeshua stifling a yawn, and urged him to take a nap in the shelter of the bow. He needed little coaxing, and grinned at his friends apologetically as he made his way to the front of the boat to lie down. John tucked a cushion under his head, and Yeshua sighed his thanks.

He never ceased to amaze and confuse this band of men whom he called his brothers and friends. They'd given up trying to anticipate what he might do or say, and there were times when his teachings were too hard for them to grasp. They were a diverse group, and when he was out of earshot, debates and discussions often raged. Why he wanted to hang out with the likes of them instead of the intellectuals and religious leaders, they could not fathom, but he seemed to desire, and even to prefer their company. As his constant companions, they knew his human side better than anyone. He needed friends he could trust, and with whom he could be himself away from the crowds.

Luke pulled out a flask of sweet wine and passed it around. The boat swayed gently in its liquid cradle, and no one spoke. Embraced by peace and bound by camaraderie, there was a silent consensus that life didn't get better than moments like these.

Peter had almost dozed off himself when the tiller suddenly jerked violently under his hand. The mainsail snapped taut as a cold blast of wind slammed into the side of the skiff, causing it to lurch violently. The men exchanged surprised looks, and Andrew shouted in alarm as he pointed toward the north. Storms were unheard of in the region this time of the year, but a dense, ominous gray wall had materialized out of nowhere and was billowing toward them. Within seconds it blocked out the sun, and then it unleashed its full fury upon the craft and her unprepared passengers.

Adrenalin shot through Peter's veins. He leapt to his feet, clamped both of his huge, rugged hands around the wildly swinging tiller and brought it under control. He was a man of action – a take-charge guy in tough situations – but he wasn't sure if his old boat could hold up under such a thrashing. He would never have suggested the trip if there'd been any threat of a storm.

One violent wave after another swamped the craft. Peter's brother Andrew and the other fishermen onboard knew what to do, but the petrified looks on the faces of the others told Peter they'd be of little help. He screamed commands at them anyway. *"Help John get that sail down! Bail! Bail!"* If they worked as a team, they might survive. They'd be thrown far off course, but all he cared about was staying afloat and not losing anyone overboard. It just figured that the first time Yeshua trusted his judgment, something like this would happen! He'd never claimed to be a very smart or spiritual man, but at least they all respected his knowledge of the sea. Terror sank its teeth into his heart as the worst case scenario filled his mind – if the boat went down, the blame would rest on him.

Water poured into the boat faster than the crew could bail. Friends who'd shared such easy companionship moments earlier now screamed at one another over the tempest, but the wind tore the words from their lips before they could be heard.

Peter strained to see through the wall of rain and stinging sea spray. He wasn't sure whether to believe his eyes, but it looked like their leader was still curled up sleeping, and the sight filled him with fresh confidence and determination. If Yeshua – who was always uncannily aware of *everything* that was going on – trusted him, shouldn't he trust himself? It was his boat, and by Jehovah, he'd get them through this crisis.

Someone yelled, *"We're going down! Wake the teacher!"*

Peter yelled back, *"No! Just bail faster! Sit down and shut up! You're rocking the boat!"*

The men glared at him and one of them called him a crude name. In defiance of Peter's orders, two of the others crawled to the bow where they shook Yeshua awake.

"Teacher! How can you be sleeping through this? Don't you know what's happening? A terrible storm has come upon us and we're all going to drown!"

Yeshua opened his eyes and looked at them with mild surprise that quickly turned to disappointment when he saw the mayhem. No fear registered on his face, but he immediately arose, grasped the rail, and thrust his right arm upward as if he were grabbing the storm by the scruff of the neck. His voice could be heard above the howling wind, and with unflinching authority, he commanded the elements themselves.

"Cease! Be at peace!"

And as the men watched in stunned disbelief, the storm obeyed. Within seconds, the wind and rain stopped, the churning sea became calm, and the black clouds rolled up and away like a curtain to reveal a deep twilight sky studded with the first evening stars. The only remaining evidence of the hurricane that had conspired to take their lives a moment earlier was the water still dripping from their drenched robes and sloshing around their feet.

The trembling, bewildered men sank to their seats and stared, dumbstruck, at the one who had just demonstrated his power over the wind and sea. They'd all witnessed it. They'd all heard him.

Yeshua searched his companions' faces. Their thoughts were always written there. Oh, how predictable they were. Would they surprise him one day? How he longed for that day! Why was it still so hard for them to believe in him? Why couldn't they see past the ends of their own noses? When would they stop allowing fear to control them? How many more signs did they need to see? When would they learn to trust him? Would they ever understand why he'd come? Why did they wait so long to ask for his help? The answer was always the same: Pride.

He sighed and put a couple of these questions to them. He didn't expect answers, but hoped to stimulate independent thought and discussion later on. Peter, of course, was quick to explain and apologize, but the others just hung their heads as they often did, and said nothing.

"You can raise the sails again, John. Don't worry, Peter, we're still on course." Yeshua lay back down, laced his fingers behind his head and fixed his eyes on the stars.

The men began a discourse in hushed tones.

Who is this man that even the wind and the sea obey him?

"This is no ordinary man. I've been telling you that since the beginning!"

"There was no way this barge was going to stay afloat much longer."

"Hey, watch what you call my old gal!" Peter countered defensively. *"She got us through."*

"Let's see...who was it that suggested this trip in the first place and said it was perfect sailing weather...oh, yeah, I remember..."

*"The weather **was** fine when I said that!"*

"Well, I'll be thinking twice before I climb aboard any boat with you at helm again, Peter! If the Master hadn't been with us we'd all be fish food by now!"

*"Did you hear him yell at the storm? What was **that**?"*

"I think this trip down the coast is getting out of hand. I mean, the crowds keep getting bigger, and now Roman soldiers and government spies are tracking us..."

"What's he going to do to stir things up next? Raise the dead?"

"Hey, Luke, is there any wine left? I'm a nervous wreck."

"Peter, I hate to ask, but do you have any idea how long it's going to be before we get to shore? I'm soaking wet and I really want out of this boat!"

అ

107

S.G.Rose

Anything I Know,
I Learned the Hard Way

You need only look into the eyes of an old saint or an old sinner, and listen to their words, to see that the hardships of this life eventually create either beauty and character – or the opposite.

❖

When we learn to be tolerant of the irritations and intrusions that find their way into our lives instead of immediately trying to expel them, we will increase our opportunity for blessing. These grating grains of sand, if embraced and patiently endured, may one day be revealed as pearls of great price.

❖

A person will do far more for the sake of love than they will ever do for the sake of duty.

❖

I used to fret over the state of all the souls whose beliefs, or lack of them, clashed with the liberating truths God had shown me. I'd open my door and my mind to those who knocked; listen and share with them; pray for them; and worry about them. Then one day God's words in the Book of Jeremiah came to life. *"...You will seek Me...and when you seek with all of your heart you will find Me."* • Jeremiah 29:13

If anyone honestly searches for God with an open heart, it's promised that the Spirit of Truth will lead them to Him. On that eternal journey, our missteps or detours serve only to make us wiser, for we're also guaranteed that all things will ultimately *"work together for our good."* I don't worry about folks anymore. • Romans 8:28

❖

"Don't miss the lunar eclipse at 7:30 tonight! It's going to be spectacular!" I'd received several reminders that day, and was

enthusiastically looking forward to the event. Clear February skies are a rarity in the Pacific Northwest, and I hadn't witnessed an eclipse in decades.

We worked until six forty-five. At seven-fifteen we sat down to dinner and turned on the TV, grateful for technology that enabled us to fast-forward and re-wind through our favorite pre-recorded shows at will. Sometime after ten, we headed upstairs.

I opened the bedroom door to find the room bathed in the ethereal glow of the full moon. Rivers of soft, silvery light streamed through the windows, spilled over the bed and flowed across the floor. The luminescence cast its romantic, heavenly spell over me, and I succumbed, only to have the blissful moment evaporate a second later when I realized, with a jolt, that in spite of all my earlier good intentions, I'd forgotten about the eclipse.

Acute disappointment displaced euphoria, and my first desperate, irrational thought was that there might be some way for me to rewind back to what I'd missed. I immediately returned to my senses, of course, but the fact that such an absurd notion had even entered my mind was cause for serious introspection.

As penance for missing His celestial spectacle, I did not ask God to forgive my forgetfulness or to soothe my disappointment by revealing some deeper meaning in what had happened. But later, as I climbed into bed and gazed out at the perfect, shining moon, He talked to me about it anyway.

Life goes by. Sunny days, starry nights, magic moments and eclipses come and go, enjoyed or missed, remembered or forgotten. Words are spoken or left unspoken, kindnesses shown or omitted, hugs given or withheld, hearts healed or hurt. God doesn't hand out universal remotes so we can fast forward through the undesirable parts or stop the action when we need a break. There's no rewind button for this once-around life.

"Blessed are those who keep their priorities in order, for they shall live with fewer regrets."

❖

Most of us can manage dying to self as long as we are sure all of the right people will attend the funeral and deliver glowing eulogies.

❖

110

Don't start a tug of war with God over your tattered old security blanket – whatever form it may take. If He's pulling it away, it's because it's time for you to grow up – and as an adult, you probably look very silly sucking on it and dragging it around with you everywhere.

❖

When we're trudging across the desert, dying of hunger and thirst in the blistering heat, the oasis is our only hope. Desperately we pray, and miraculously, it materializes. With our last ounce of strength we crawl in and are saved. There, we rest, eat, drink, heal, and slowly recover. We thank God and vow to Him that we will never wander away from the shelter of His arms again.

But inevitably, our memory of the fear and desolation we felt when we were lost in sin begins to fade. We forget the bitter loneliness and the agony of our life-or-death struggle.

Foolish, restless, reckless wanderers. We've barely recovered and we're already taking the oasis for granted.

❖

Lord, grant that those who plaster their bumpers with Christian slogans can live what they preach when they're in rush hour traffic. ~Amen

❖

Life's most crushing sorrows alter our substance forever. Within the dust and blood that remain, elements previously hidden are exposed – new materials with which God can create richer life, if they are surrendered to His hand.

Precious minerals within the stone; wine within the grapes; humility within a human heart. These are not revealed any other way but through the crushing process.

❖

The promises of God's Word are like checks made out to us on an infinite bank account, but until we sign our name and take them to the bank, they're nothing but ink and paper.

❖

111

(A Paradox: Those who scoff at Godly faith would do well to observe themselves objectively for just one day, and they'd see that they actively practice faith every waking moment. They have faith that they will wake up in the morning; faith that sun will rise; faith that the paper will be on their doorstep; faith that the electricity will flow to their lights, furnace, coffee maker, television and computer; faith that the kitchen chair won't collapse beneath them; faith that hot water will pour from the shower; faith that their car will start. They can't tell me they don't need faith. They just place theirs in things a lot less dependable than the Creator of the Universe.)

❖

(Another Paradox) The trendy spiritual gurus who dismiss Christianity as an "archaic religion," along with the notion of Jesus as the Son of God and the Savior of mankind.

One such individual was showcased on a popular television program that boasts an international viewing audience of millions.

"Jesus was not the Son of God who came to die for the sins of the world," he patiently explained. *"There is no sin. Jesus is merely representative of the Christ within each of us."*

The point was that "enlightened" people need not ever again be burdened with the question of sin, repentance, or what to do with the actual *person* of Jesus Christ. So, it would follow (for the logical thinker) that the faith of countless souls over the ages was and is misplaced, and billions were and are, deluded. It was high time, he urged, for us to leave the dark ages and hoist ourselves up to a higher level of consciousness.

The guru and the host were *so* sincere. So genuine. So calm. So rational. So *convincing.* They were spiritually minded, kind, generous, fulfilled, famous, prosperous, and didn't need "saving." None of us do, they soothed. We just need an attitude adjustment. Jesus was, after all, not a *real* man. He is just a symbol, an archetype, a myth – like Zeus.

I couldn't wait to hear the other life-altering revelations I suspected would be forthcoming after the commercial break for cat litter, volumizing mascara, and a heartburn pill with the risk of potentially lethal side-effects.

"And we're back. ...so, what about Heaven?" the host asked the guru. *"Do you believe in it?"*

112

"Jesus said, 'the Kingdom of Heaven is within you,'" he replied. *Whoa!* Wait a minute. Back up the bus! Did he just quote the same Jesus he'd declared was a *myth* before the station break? Surely I wasn't the only one who'd caught that. There had to be a hand waving frantically somewhere in the studio audience to beg the question of how you can quote someone who never existed.

I held my breath and waited for the rousing debate that was bound to ensue – the throwing down of the gauntlet by some Champion of the Faith who would rise from their seat to challenge this guy.

The camera panned across the rows of well-groomed, mannerly folk, but there was no hand in the air – at least none that I could see. Perhaps the audience had been pre-screened before being admitted, or told they had to check their beliefs and common sense at the door. They appeared mesmerized by the guru's claims, and many were nodding in glassy-eyed agreement. Jesus would have called them *"Sheep without a shepherd."* • Mark 6:34 When people came to hear Him speak, He taught them, comforted them, fed them, healed them and ultimately died for their sins and stupidity. He gave them hope, faith, a foundation and eternal life. The crowds following this guy were not so fortunate.
• Matthew 9:36

I had no desire to watch the remainder of the program, but I'd bank on the fact that the guru was not heard quoting the words of "myth Jesus" in Matthew 7:15, *"Beware of false prophets who come to you in sheep's clothing..."*

❖

There is never anyone we succeed in deceiving more craftily than ourselves.

❖

Wisdom from a four-year-old in the midst of a lunch food fight with his sibling:

Mom (through gritted teeth, standing in kitchen with peanut butter knife in hand): *"All right, you kids! I told you to knock it off, and now I've lost my patience!"*

Child (wide-eyed with genuine, serious concern): *"Oh-oh! You **lost** 'em? Well just grabum real quick and put them back in your mouth! Do you need me to help you findum, Mama?"*

113

❖

In my early years as a Believer, I attended a number of different churches. They had a guilt-producing label for people like me: *Church Hopper.* But to disobey the leading of the Spirit would have felt far worse than being hammered with *"We missed you last Sunday...where were you?"* And, further down the road I could always look back and clearly see why God had moved me on.

Some independent fellowships had begun with a pure directive but evolved sideways into something else. Change was less likely (or at least took longer) in the mainstream denominations, but established doctrines discouraged individual spiritual growth. Conditions were prevalent everywhere. Our society is already overburdened with laws and requirements – who wants more? I guess some folks must (the ones who make them), but I'm a rebel with a cause. The truth has set me free and I'm not about to give up that freedom.

Jesus said, *"My sheep know my voice and they follow me...a stranger's voice they will not follow...I call them by name and lead them out...I lead them in, and out, and to find pasture."* That sounds like a lot of moving around with the Shepherd to me.

The sheep analogy can take you down some interesting roads of thought, especially if you've lived on a ranch, as I did for a time. While fluffy and cute, sheep aren't very smart. They like the safety of numbers and don't appear to know what's best for them, so it's relatively easy for men and dogs to round them up and fence them in. Once contained, they can be counted, controlled, fleeced or slaughtered, depending upon the rancher's agenda.

The bigger the flock, the richer the rancher, providing he has a good business sense. Plenty of grain and amenities keep the sheep content and growing fatter. Before long, they need a larger corral and more ranch hands, which must be paid for, of course, with greater quantities of fleece and flesh. And so on it goes.

Those who misappropriate the title of Shepherd, and set themselves in positions of authority over God's children are usurping power He's never given them. Jesus is the *only* Shepherd and we are *all* *"...the sheep of his pasture."* He does not command dogs to herd and control us – He *leads* us, and the choice to follow Him is ours. That's a picture of complete freedom under *His* loving, watchful care.

My wanderings have taught me to get up and follow my Shepherd whenever He calls, whether the rest of the flock does so or not.

If they are lying around cold and miserable in the ruts of a field where the grass has been eaten down to dry stubble, and Jesus is pointing to a lush green pasture over the next hill, I'm not going to stay there and starve with them just to keep them company.

If they're lined up nose-to-tail in the shearing chute, and Jesus whistles from the other side of the pen where He's holding the gate open, I'm heading *that* way. And, should they bleat accusingly at me when I trot into the wilderness by His side, the only thing they'll hear this black sheep say is, *"good-baa-aaa."* • John 10

❖

When we have been emotionally wounded, the speed with which we heal will be solely dependent upon our own capacity for love, mercy and forgiveness. Only when those forces flow through us without reservation, from God to *"those who trespassed against us,"* can our own healing process begin. The power and the decision to end the pain, to bury it, or to hold on to it are contingent upon nothing and no one but ourselves. This is the stretching process of love. • *The Source*

❖

The hardest battles are fought in the heart.

❖

It is entirely appropriate for any thinking person to evaluate and form opinions based upon facts and experience. But Jesus warns against judging another. An opinion (like a person) can change, but a judgment – unless it is kind – is binding, and always carries with it conditions and punishment.

❖

Confidence and pride are vastly different, but the line between the two is fine, and often blurry.

❖

Whatever is worth doing – do it with grace.

❖

Most of us were taught to color inside the lines and not to stray from recipes, formulas, rules or traditions, lest the end product not turn out as prescribed. Unquestioning compliance rewards us with a fairly predictable outcome. But following a model or instructions develops skill, not creativity. To experience the thrill of original thought and discovery, we must follow our instincts and push the boundaries.

God cannot be contained. Observe the glorious chaos of nature. Creativity is a Divine, curious spark given to us all, even when it lies dormant in many who insist they don't have it. When fanned, this spark ignites the burning desire for something uniquely our own.

Creativity is spontaneous, fearless, uninhibited and messy – just like Creation. We can give expression to this gift by allowing ourselves to be challenged and inspired by whatever is presented to us rather than constrained by it. Observe and ask, *"What if...?"*

❖

Just as siblings within a family each have distinctly unique relationships with a shared parent, so it is with us and our Heavenly Father. God gives no one the permission to judge or dictate another soul's connection to Him, or to determine His will for another individual's life.

As God's children, our focus needs to be upon deepening our *own* relationship with the Father, and on encouraging and nurturing the same in others so that they are able to discern His will for their own lives.

There is a place for giving and receiving Godly counsel – *when it's sought* – but it comes with accountability to the Father for the repercussions. Too often, prayer requests become fodder for gossips, and the course of lives is changed by the meddling of busybodies who hide behind masks of concern.

In light of the above, it doesn't seem likely that The Almighty takes kindly to the actions of those in positions of leadership who abuse the trust people place in them by deciding what's best for, requiring the submission of, and thereby oppressing those whom they claim to serve.

"But I tell you that men will have to give account on the Day of Judgment for every careless word they have spoken." • Jesus, Matthew 12:36

❖

For those who follow Jesus, the best is *always* yet to come.

❖

The first one to forgive wins.

❖

"God changes not," but this world and our circumstances inevitably do. We can be adaptable and innovative while still retaining our values. There's a big difference between tenacity and rigidity.

❖

Personal growth requires complete honesty, and the courage to admit to and take full responsibility for one's actions, i.e., *accountability*.

The word "mistake" denotes an innocent blunder committed in ignorance or awkwardness. We all make them on occasion. Others generally respond empathetically – and hopefully, everyone learns.

Beware the habit of excusing and discounting consciously bad decisions and destructive choices by labeling them "mistakes" – as though there was no awareness of the risks or potential for harm at the time. The offenders are never the sole victims of their own foolishness and enabling them by pretending they didn't know what they were doing only ensures painful repeat performances for everyone involved.

❖

The immediate answer to a great many of our prayers is *"Look within."* We just prefer to look without. We want someone else to do the work, the changing, or the rescuing, so we delude ourselves into believing that God hasn't answered us.

Jesus didn't leave us alone and helpless when He returned to the Father. He sent the Holy Spirit to live within us, to teach us, comfort us and empower us to carry on His work? His parting assurance was, *"Truly I tell all of you with certainty, the one who believes in me will also do what I am doing. He will do even greater things than these, because I am going to the Father."* • John 14:12

What more do we want Him to give us or do for us? We're fully equipped and the power is switched on. What remains?

We are often the answer to our own prayers. We are accountable for the knowledge we've received, and we are Jesus' hands, feet, heart and mind on the earth, now. He wants partners, not legions of lazy

117

whiners. It's long past time to shake off all latency, pick up the tools He's given us, and get to work. ✝ Colossians 1:24-39

❖

Let us die to self daily; be born again daily; repent daily; be forgiven daily; pray and listen daily; be taught and learn daily; give and receive daily; love and be loved daily. Awakening to and walking with God is not a one-time event – it's a minute-by-minute, growing, evolving, deepening *relationship*.

❖

No kindness is small.

❖

My youngest son was a fearless, adventuresome toddler with escape skills. One summer day, he and his brother accompanied me on a visit to my friend Cheryl's house, where, immediately upon our arrival, they were invited to go to a playground with her son and several other children. The neighborhood was surrounded by acres of forest, and the play area was in a ravine a quarter-mile away. The trail was too steep for a two-year-old, so while the rest of the gang ran noisily out the door, one extremely unhappy little fellow was told he needed to stay with Mommy.

Moments later, Cheryl and I became engrossed in conversation and the wily tyke seized the opportunity to make his getaway. By the time I noticed he was no longer playing with the toys in the corner of the room, he was long gone. When we couldn't find him in the house or yard, our search turned frantic. I feared and suspected that he'd gone into the woods to look for the older kids.

We ran to the playground, but no one had seen him. While my friend organized a posse of neighbor children to canvas the large, sprawling housing development, I grabbed my five-year-old son by the hand and we began to search the surrounding forest. I fought frightening visions of his little brother wandering alone through the treacherous terrain, and struggled not to panic. As we ran through the maze of trails, climbed over logs and skirted deep holes that had been dug for septic systems, we alternated between crying out his name, and praying together out loud, *"Jesus, please help us find him! Please send Your angels to protect him, and keep him safe!"*

118

It was impossible to maintain our bearings, and before long, we were lost. It was past noon before the trail we were on abruptly led out of the woods into an unfamiliar cul-de-sac. I breathed my thanks to God, and when a tired, worried little voice asked, *"What do we do now, Mommy?"* I could only reply, *"We'll just have to keep walking until we figure out where we are."*

I was considering knocking on someone's door to ask if I could use their phone, when three children emerged from behind a house and ran toward us shouting, *"We found him! We found him!"* We raced back with them to Cheryl's home, where a small crowd had gathered in the driveway. The chubby toddler at its center looked none the worse for wear, and seemed bewildered by the excitement his return had caused.

I fell to my knees, threw my arms around him, smothered him with kisses, and said all the things a distraught, incredibly relieved mother would say. *"My baby, my baby...are you okay? Why did you go out into the woods by yourself? We looked everywhere for you...and we prayed and prayed and Jesus heard us and He found you!"*

He looked at me curiously and corrected me in toddler-speak. *"Jesus didn't find me. An angel did. Den she took me to dose kids."* He pointed at the three who had run to us.

*"An **angel** found you?"*

He nodded emphatically, as though I should have known.

Unable to resist extracting more detail from this little one whose eyes could still see Heavenly hosts, I asked the obvious question and held my breath: *"What did the angel look like?"*

His matter-of-fact answer had a tone of finality that told me further interrogation would be fruitless. *"She was green."*

≈

(Update: The boy is now a man, but he's still fearless, still forges his own path regardless of the obstacles, and still encounters angels.)

❖

Great or small, good deeds still speak
long after we have earned our sleep,
and should there be no earthly praise
what matters that in Heaven's Days?
When angels applaud our arrival home
and God smiles and says, *"My child, well done!"*

❖

Risk takers generally live with fewer regrets, and if they have them, they aren't the sort that begin with *"I've always wished I'd..."*

❖

Deanna was my shop manager, a perfectionist, and ran the crew like a drill sergeant. Each gift item off of the assembly line met her rigid standards and she squeezed every penny like it was her own. I was blessed to have her. The recession of the early 80's was affecting everyone, and we were all struggling.

Deanna marched her starched, pressed family to church every Sunday, but for all her outward strength and pride, I knew the truth: she tortured herself with fear, worry and doubt. I encouraged her daily to trust the God Who had never failed me, and cited His miracles and promises of provision, but my words were like water off a duck's back.

One December night, Deanna had bundled up to walk home, but a storm was brewing, so I offered to give her a ride. She'd been fretful all day, as usual. Her car was in the shop, they were low on groceries, Christmas was coming – and there was never enough money. Her tone was sarcastic as she reminded me of my assurances that God would provide, and pointed out that He obviously wasn't doing so. She didn't *"get it."* Should she pray *harder*? Was she not being *specific* enough?

"He already knows what you need," I replied. *"I wish you could believe that."* Her face told me she could not. I knew she'd been abused by her father as a child. I knew, too, that her Heavenly Father saw her pain, and longed for her to allow Him to love her better.

We drove in silence through the dark, empty streets. I'd just turned a corner when we were startled by the sight of pieces of paper flying up in front of the headlights. *"Deanna!"* I exclaimed incredulously, *"That looked like money!"* I slammed on the brakes, threw the car into reverse and backed up. For a second we both stared in shock at the bills skittering across the pavement in the wind, and then I excitedly urged her, *"Hurry! Go get it before it blows away!"*

Deanna jumped out, chased the money down, and climbed back in the car with a stupefied look on her face and a large wad of twenty-dollar bills clutched in her hand. There were no houses nearby and no cars in sight. Speechlessly, she held the bills out toward me.

"Oh, no." I shook my head and laughed, *"I'm absolutely positive that's meant for **you**."*

120

Needless to say, I never had to preach to Deanna about God's provision again.

❖

"Store your treasures in Heaven, where moth and dust do not destroy..." and where the third-generation family heirloom crystal cake stand entrusted to you for safekeeping will not slip from your hands and shatter into a million pieces on the floor after you've told your sweet young granddaughter that it was *sooo* special, fragile and valuable that it would be best for *you* to carry it. • Matthew 6:19-21

❖

Me (frustrated): *"Lord, this is too hard! I have no clue how to do it. There are countless others out there who are infinitely better qualified. They're smarter, skilled, educated. I struggle and feel inadequate every step of the way. You* **must** *have people who could do this easier than me!"*

Him: *"Well, that may be true, but I didn't ask one of them to do it, did I? I asked you."* • II Corinthians 2:10

❖

Don't underestimate your impact on your neighborhood, town, county, state, country, or the world. Jesus never traveled more than two hundred miles from His place of birth, and He had no Internet access.

❖

Every moment of every hour of every day we are forming habits. Consciously or unconsciously, we are programming ourselves, and our hearts, minds, bodies and souls will conform. *How* we choose to shape ourselves is completely up to us. Freedom of will = *Power*

All evidence appears to point to the fact that this is the way the Creator manages His creation...by setting it in motion, and then keeping a watchful eye on the Divine order within the chaos. It would seem to follow that since we came to the planet endowed with free will, we'll also have it when we leave.

We are eternal beings who've been given the power to affect our own destinies, and whether we're consciously aware of it or not, we're continually investing in and preparing for the life after this one. In a sense, each of us has been granted the liberty to design our own hereafter. Because this freedom too often results in darkness and suffering, we are offered the Light – and again, we're free to accept or reject it.   • Isaiah 9:2

Perhaps, when we step into the next realm, we will find exactly that which we most loved, desired, focused on and worked hardest for here on earth: Heaven…or something else.

❖

We achieve nothing by raging against what is happening around us. Understanding our own place in the picture is the key to changing it.

❖

The greatest gift we can ever give or receive is unconditional love.

❖

One night I had a frightening dream where I was confined in a small, dark place and trying desperately to escape. Walls pressed in on me from every side, severely restricting my movement. My body felt alarmingly frail and weak, and I could only push forward by feel. Every move exhausted what little strength I had, and I was forced to rest before pressing on. I was disoriented and terrified but giving up was not an option. My instincts screamed that this was a life-or-death struggle, and I wanted desperately to live. I didn't know what would be waiting for me – only that if I was to survive, I had to get out.

Progress was excruciatingly slow, but somehow I kept going – and then, with one final heroic push, I entered this world.

The hardest thing we will ever have to do, we have already done.

≈

(This is not to exempt all the c-section babies, for whom the birth experience is different, but by no means less traumatic!)

❖

Open your heart and hands to give, and Heaven will continually re-fill them. You cannot out-give God.

❖

The church is God's emergency room.

122

❖

Love's highest purpose is not always to rescue and comfort us – but to challenge us, teach us, humble us, heal us and change us.

❖

It's vital to our mental and spiritual health to forgive those who have hurt us, whether they seek it or not. But how do we deal with our lingering emotions?

I genuinely believed I'd forgiven a person who had caused me much pain and sorrow, but instead of the peace and healing that act should have brought, my mind remained in a state of unrest. Like a caged hamster addicted to its wheel, I'd daily chase the same questions of *"How?"* and *"Why?"* to the point of mental and emotional exhaustion. Some relentless P.I. within my psyche was bent upon making sense of what had happened, and demanded resolution where none existed.

The individual in question was no longer in my life, so why was I still fighting this battle? Each torturous mental session drug me backward into heartbreaking events that I wanted to forget, and no logical answers ever surfaced. At the end of each fruitless exercise, I'd conclude that I must not have forgiven well enough in the first place, and so would perform the ritual again. This painful routine continued for years, until the blessed day that God, The Great Psychologist, said to my heart, *"Letting go is a form of forgiveness."*

Could it *be* that easy? I was desperate, so immediately put it to the test. I abandoned the unanswerable questions, relinquished any right or need to know the answers, informed the inner detective that we were *dropping* the case, and *released* the person. And when I did so, I was set free. It really *was* that easy. *...Let go of the string.*

❖

Live and love in the moment, for each precious moment is followed by the next, and together, they add up to *Forever.*

❖

We are not just Believers in the Divine Plan. We *are* the Divine Plan.

❖

123

S.G.Rose

Instructions

Help me, Lord,
to hear Your voice
when You speak.

I once was sure
I heard quite well
but these days
I'm beginning to see
I'm not as sainted
as I thought –
and sometimes
I'm a bit hard of listening.

Maybe if You could wave a flag
from Heaven
when You whisper,
and I'm not paying attention.
Or ring a bell
when You speak through someone else
and I'm busy talking.
How about an angel to blow a trumpet
and shout my name
if it's me You want.

Or better yet,
send me a letter,
Certified
Return Receipt Requested,
with detailed instructions
so I do this all right?

◆

Proverbs 8:32-35

S.G.Rose

metamorphosis   *a little tale*

i tell you I'm fine, living day to day,
        i don't understand what you're trying to say.
i'm perfectly happy just inching along,
        no illusions of grandeur, so what could go wrong?
i have lots of friends who all creep along too,
        we've got places to go and things to do.
what makes you think you should preach to me?
        we're both merely insects, so just let me be!
i'm quite satisfied and know where i belong,
        don't fret about me – please just run along.
your sermons, my friend, are too hard to believe…
        that we creatures can fly – well i just don't agree.
all that matters to me, i can taste, touch and smell,
        so what makes you think i'm not living life well?
i don't expect more than this earth to see –
        your stories are foolish – they're fantasy.
a reality check's what you need, I fear –
        why can't you accept that it's just like this here?
i'm tired of you bugging me, i've heard it all,
        i'm closing my ears, rolling up in a ball.
and don't come around here 'cause i'm moving soon
        see i got this strange urge to spin a cocoon.
don't get all excited, it's not what it seems
        i still don't believe in that "born again" thing.
please don't knock again, i won't answer the door
        i know you mean well but you're making me snore.
i have other things on my mind, you know
        did you notice the weather's grown terribly cold?
just live your own life and i'll deal with mine
        i'd like to be alone now if you don't mind.
thanks for your concern, let me shake your hand
        g'bye, i need a nap, hope you understand.

                ◆

in my dream i was drifting and gliding somewhere…
        it all felt so real, i could swear i was there!

didn't want to wake up, have the joy slip away
        but i've overslept, gotta face a new day.
i don't know how, but this house sure got small
        and a draft's coming in from that crack in the wall.
i need to get out of here, stretch and be free
        hey, something's changed – what's happened to me?
i have wings! and they're beautiful! look at me *fly!*
        i guess i was wrong to doubt that guy
when he said that faith could conquer the night,
        and if i believed, I'd be born in the light...
that earthbound no more, I could live in the skies
        and see the world through different eyes.
i'd lied when i told him that I didn't mind
        my miserable life in the dirt with my kind.
i was just saving face, didn't want him to see
        that i ached for a miracle i could believe.
when he was gone and i laid down my head,
        i couldn't forget the words he'd said.
i breathed a prayer ... 'twas hope's last sigh
        and gave my will to One higher than i.

◆

i can't wait to go and show all of my friends
        how much I've changed from what i was then.
i hope they listen when i try to tell them

        that they never

        have to crawl

        again.

◆
II Corinthians 5:17
◆

128

Matthew 7:7-8

Along with other artistic pursuits, I worked as a calligrapher for many years. I loved lettering Scripture the most – adding flourishes, illustrations, and illuminating the first character of each verse, as was commonly done in ancient manuscripts.

One day, I felt moved to inscribe Jesus' powerful promises of the verse below. Not until the piece was completed did I notice He had added His own emphasis.

A sk   ~ and it shall be given to you.

S eek ~ and you shall find.

K nock ~ and the door shall be opened.

❧ A S K ☙

S.G.Rose

Solitary Heart

Solitary heart ~ in moments like these
when old comforts call your name,
look back down on your cage and remember the day
the door swung open on sheltered captive past.

The rusted lock hangs useless now

on that empty prison.
No man can keep you there,
for I gave you the key when you cried to Me,
and broke the chains that bound you, My child.

You have always belonged to the stars, you know ~

I smiled when you spread your anxious wings
and flew.
Old streets lie beneath you now,
yesterday's house crumbles far below.
Turn your face, fair spirit, and come follow Me
I have only begun to teach you this sky!
Come higher,
Look wider,

Fly on, fly on!

Fragile new Phoenix, wings of silver and gold

clothed with knowledge
you are young ~ you are old.
Beautiful soul, grown wise and strong
from the ashes, *ARISE!*

Fly on, fly on!

Climb ever upward 'til you kiss the Son,
this new flight is eternal ~ your song, your home.
Embrace each horizon
for they mark well your course,
touch those there with your magic, and then

Fly on.

Rest only lightly

if when weary you must,
lest earth's tethers bind you
to that which is dust.
Shake off your slumber
but hold fast to your dream,
feast on the Truth ~
and trust, Angel, trust.

Solitary heart ~ fear not the pain

you are one with Tomorrow,
each loss become gain.

Search never ending, yet destiny known.

I am flying beside you ~
you are never alone.

≈

Matthew 28:19-20

Dragons & Dungeons

"OH....GOD!" The agonizing wail rattled the gates of Heaven, and the attending angel shook his head sadly. Billions of prayers ascended from Planet Earth every instant of the day, week, month, year, decade and millennium, but some had a particularly desperate tone that set them apart. He'd have waged his wings that the cry for help was dragon-related. One of them had another human in its clutches.

Thankfully, the King believed in a hands-on approach, and answered every call from His creations personally. Warrior angels would be dispatched – he always looked forward to pulling that duty himself, and the chance to kick demon tail – but even though they would go to battle for this soul, it was going to take more than that to win the war.

He didn't question His Majesty's mercy and love for these beings, but he couldn't understand their determination to walk straight into the same pitfalls they'd been warned about for thousands of years. He sighed and reminded himself that it was not his place to ponder that enigma. His assignment, today, was to transmit communications to the throne room, and it was all he could do to keep up.

As the angel fine-tuned the channel, the anguished cry came in more clearly, this time punctuated by moans and sobs.

"GOD! I hope You can hear me! I've got a really big problem! There's an angry creature hiding deep down inside, and...well...I've been hoping it would just go away...I know it heard me tell it to leave...but it just now came slithering up from the pit again, spewing fire and destroying everything in it's path...oh, God, I can't even predict when it's going to rear its ugly head anymore! I never knew this thing was going to get so cruel and out of hand when I brought it home!"

The pathetic soul paused in the recital of its petition, sniffled, blew its nose, tried to calm itself, and continued in a slightly more rational tone, which the angel knew signaled Stage II (negotiation).

"Okay...well...to be honest, I knew the little critter looked sorta like a dragon when I picked it up, but I was sure I could control it, You know? I've been careful to keep it out of sight down in the dungeon, and most of the time its pretty content to lie down there in its cell and sleep. Sometimes I even forget its there...until somebody bothers it. Why can't

133

they just leave it alone?" (The pathetic weeping began again.) *"I swear, they start coaxing and teasing and testing it, and if that doesn't get a response, they start prodding and pushing and provoking it until it wakes up. Oh, God...the roaring, the trashing, the spewing! It's a horrible sight...but maybe You've seen it. I'm humiliated and tormented by this thing!*

"God...I don't know what to do. That's why I called You. I don't want it here anymore, but I've tried everything and it refuses to leave! Somebody told me a long time ago that I should ask You to send the Prince to slay it, but I'm embarrassed to say that I thought I was smart enough to handle the situation myself, and, well...I have to admit that back then I was kinda attached to it. Now, I know it has to go. I hate it and the misery it's caused me and all the people I care about. I just want peace...and control over my own life again! God...I'm so scared that it might already be too late! Help me, please!"

More heart-wrenching sobs signaled the end of the prayer, and the angel hit the *Send* button. The King would have the answer, but a lot of these praying folks could be a bit hard of hearing when it came to His directions. They'd been given a detailed instruction manual long ago, but somewhere along the way they'd gotten the notion that it was outdated, subject to individual interpretation and took too long to read. So, most of them didn't consult it much. Something in their nature seemed to compel them to learn everything the hard way instead. Then, after they'd made a mess of it, they wanted the King to fix it for them. Maybe it was time for another bulletin. He decided to put a note in the suggestion box. It couldn't hurt.

❖

GUIDE FOR DRAGON OWNERS

Due to a high volume of urgent calls from My children, I, your King, am issuing this *Special Report*.

Recent studies reveal that mankind's thinking has finally evolved to the level where many more of you are willing to admit to your dragons than in ages past. Even more promising is that you are asking Me how to get rid of them. I am very pleased with this positive trend, and since those two steps are the bravest, I anticipate a dramatic increase in successful dragon exterminations.

Petitions for Divine deliverance are still being accepted, of course, and will always receive My personal attention, but the following Do-It-Yourself instructions have been compiled as an effective alternative to instantaneous, miraculous eradication, if you previously thought that was your only hope.

HOW TO REMOVE AN UNWANTED DRAGON

STEP I:
Do not visit the dungeon for conversations with the dragon. It will begin to wonder what's going on upstairs, and may get edgy when it's ignored. Take no notice of this. Put your mind on higher things...call Me or message Me any time of the night or day. We'll chat.

STEP II:
Do not allow anyone else to visit the dungeon. No dragon is tame and you can only expect the worst if yours is awakened. It will smell a meal, and lives for such visits.

STEP III:
Do play soothing music and read positive inspirational verse over the intercom. This will have a hypnotic effect on the beast and will keep it subdued much of the time.

STEP IV: *(The importance of this point cannot be overemphasized!)*
Do not feed the dragon. You will probably find this difficult, since it's been your pet for so long. You both have a routine and you can expect to hear it moan when you don't deliver its favorite morsels on cue. It needs fuel to continue its reign of terror, and even the smallest scrap will give it strength. *Do not give in to its demands!*

STEP V:
Do remember who the master is. *You* have the power to control the beast and its destiny. The hungrier it becomes, the more you may feel its

depression seeping up from the dungeon to cloud your thoughts. It will remind you of everything the two of you have been through together. It will list all of those who ever did you wrong and deserve to feel its wrath. It will tell you that you can't get along without it and that you need to keep it around for protection. It will coax you, tempt you, threaten you, and do everything within its power to drag you back down to the dungeon to wallow with it in self pity. It's a liar. Do not listen. Go outside, walk somewhere beautiful, breathe, and allow the beauty of My realm to fill your soul...or jump on the treadmill...or create a piece of art ...or write Me a letter...or sign up for a class. You get the idea.

STEP VI:
Do focus on the *facts*, regardless of what you see, hear or feel. Remind yourself of the destruction and torment the dragon caused and make a list of the reasons you want it gone from your life. Its elimination is simply a process, and *you* control that process. Realize that dragons die slowly by this method, but eventually yours will grow silent. You might even forget it's down there.

STEP VII:
Don't forget about the dragon! Have a cremation celebration with no one in attendance but yourself. Don't prepare a self-deprecating eulogy detailing the morbid past, and don't save any ashes.

STEP VIII:
Do immediately renovate the dungeon. Knock down all the interior walls, haul away all the rubbish you've been holding onto for years and install big windows. Make some new friends who don't know how it used to look, and throw a party.

STEP IX:
Do invite the Prince over for dinner and a private tour. He enjoys such occasions immensely and will happily accept. He'll praise you for a project well done and will probably point out that while swift swords and magic wands are nice to wish for, all the power you needed was within you from the start, and that He was watching and applauding your progress the whole time, even when you questioned whether or not you were making any. He'll also reassure you that although you regret

wasting so many years wallowing with the dragon, the passage of Earth time has never meant anything in Our kingdom to begin with, and all those myths about it being too late to start over just aren't true.

STEP X:
Do be patient with yourself and others. Those who felt the dragon's fire in the past may not believe it is really gone. Ask their forgiveness. Show them kindness. Love them unconditionally. Give them, and yourself, time to heal. Be willing to let them go if that is their choice.

STEP XI:
Do count yourself wiser and stronger for having overcome the dragon. Move forward, and live in the Now. Share what you learned.

WARNING ♦ WARNING ♦ WARNING

As the dragon population grows, so does availability. If you are tempted to bring home one of these deceitful creatures in its infancy, stop to consider the long-range consequences of your decision first. It will not remain small or cute for long. It's been bred to dig in its claws and feed upon your weakness until it rules you, and the more time you spend with it the bigger it will get. Every dragon, without exception, grows into a ravenous, unpredictable, devious monster whose destructive traits will ultimately poison its owner.

A partial list of warning signs follows. If any of these conditions are present, seek My help immediately.

Self-righteousness	Pettiness	Criticism
Blame	Vindictiveness	Anger
Vengefulness	Cruelty	Bitterness
Greed	Selfishness	Lust
Haughtiness	Pride	Hatred

And/or denial of any or all of the above.

᷾

S.G.Rose

The Temple

Spirit...

how much of this house
do You call home?

I hear You knocking on the locked doors;

I've drawn the curtains,
closed the shutters against Your light,
left stairways unfinished,
and the cellar's a scary place.

Too often this house

has grown cold and dark,
uninviting, untidy, unhealthy –
not fit to be called
the dwelling place of God.

Yet You've never moved out.

How can this flesh ever be worthy

of Your presence?
Only in its eventual death
shall we escape these crumbling walls, You and I.

Until then

You hand me tools
and work beside me
as we rennovate
our temple.

"Don't you know that you are the temple of God
and that the Spirit of God dwells in you?" ✦ *I Corinthians 3:16*

139

S.G.Rose

140

Compassion

$\mathcal{I}$ see the sorrow

etched on so many souls —
the hopelessness and pain in vacant faces.
How it grieves Me, the Father Who gave them life.
They believe they can never be free
of the burdens that bend their weary backs
and cripple their wounded minds.
Hypnotized by lies,
they have given up hope.

$\mathcal{P}$ rofessional sufferers view the Light

with mistrust and fear.
They have locked themselves in prisons
where they cower in the dark
and by thought and deed
unwittingly create the calamities
they dread shall befall them.

$\mathcal{S}$ o quick to conceive and bear

poisonous fruits of bitterness, anger, revenge,
they hold their demons dear.
To watch them, one might almost believe
they thrive on misery.
Yet how can this be
when they place so much worth
on the Pursuit of Happiness?

$\mathcal{O}$ h, My child,

you have not forgotten
the sorrows of the pit

141

from which you were redeemed.
Those whose lessons have been learned
at the feet of forgiveness
do not judge.

*T*ell them for Me

that they can be lifted, too!
That the power they think they have lost
lies still within their own hands
and that with their words
they build or tear down their world
each moment, as they command it to be.

*T*ell them that their battle

will be won in surrender.

*I*n release they shall receive.

*A*nd that the only price they will ever have to pay

is one they can all afford –
simply,

to *B*elieve.

❧

Baptism

I'm ashamed to admit that I wasn't expecting a very exciting evening when I accepted a friend's invitation to a prayer meeting one day. As it turned out, I couldn't have been more wrong. These folks believed in the literal truth of Jesus' promise, *"...Where two or more are gathered in my name, there I am in the midst of them..."* and they typically saw demonstrations of the power in those words. • Matthew 20:18-20

The group's practice was simply to join their hearts in praise to God. He would then lead them in the direction their prayers should take. This submission to the Spirit was far different from anything I'd known traditionally, and so were its results. For the first time, I would experience the amazing power that can link us together in perfect unity and purpose when we call upon it and yield to it.

Our shared words of praise drew us together in spirit. This was beautiful and uplifting, but it was only a prelude to what followed. We'd invited God, and the connection had been made. The sense of His presence grew stronger with each passing moment and before long, a common thread began to emerge within the prayers. One person would begin a thought, another would add to it, and so forth as we each felt inspired. Holy energy filled the room and the focus of the prayers became clear. We were being led to pray for a spiritual awakening of souls that would sweep across the earth.

If that sounds like a big order, it didn't seem so then. When we allow God's thoughts to fill our minds, it changes our perspective. Nothing is too big and nothing is impossible. That is how He sees it, because He is able to bring it about. Through prayer, we, His sons and daughters, join with Him in His work.

Suddenly, a dramatic picture, along with the words, *"This is the 'latter rain' of My Spirit upon the earth,"* appeared in my mind. I saw a mighty torrent falling from the heavens, but the downpour was not made of raindrops. Instead, countless silver needles of energy streaked toward earth, each with a unique, distinct intelligence imprinted by God for a specific destination. When they reached their precise targets, they pierced straight to the heart with laser-like accuracy, and transmitted their power.

As I marveled at the vision, I heard exclamations from around the room. Others were receiving similar messages from God. Each of us shared what we'd been shown, and we remained in that flow of oneness for some time as He continued to speak to us through one another. He assured us that He was already answering our prayers and that the rain of His Spirit was falling. We'd been given eyes to see this powerful outpouring, but an even greater deluge was still yet to come.

"It shall be as it was in the days of Noah. My rain shall once again cover the entire earth – but not by the forces of nature – by the force of My Spirit.

In Noah's day, men ignored My warnings to prepare. They trusted their own gods instead, and cared only about the gratification of their flesh. They did not seek Me, listen to Me, or commune with Me. Noah suffered their mockery for heeding and obeying Me. When the floodwaters came upon them from every direction, they awoke and sought escape, but it was too late. Their age had come to an end.

When My rain falls upon the earth in the last days, it shall seek you all, and as it was in Noah's time, there will be nowhere to hide. But the reverse shall be true as it was then. Those who have prayed for and waited for My rain will welcome it and run into the flood of My Spirit with great joy. They will not seek to be spared from this power, and they shall be saved within its tide.

I wish for no man, woman or child to be kept from this flood. I will call every soul into the rain. Those with open ears and humble hearts will hear My voice and heed My words above the voices of flesh. Immersed in the latter rain of My Spirit, they will find their eternal life."

"Then shall we know; if we follow on to know the Lord:
His going forth is prepared as the morning, and he shall come unto us as the rain
as the latter and former rain unto the earth."
•

Hosea 6:3

"As it was in the days of Noah, so it will be at the coming of the Son of Man."
•

Matthew 24:37-38

Willing

When understanding is beyond our power
and fairness turns its back on the cry of the innocent...
When justice twists,
and crowns the victim with pain...
When the love we seek wears a deaf disguise
and our hearts ache with confusion...
When bitterness demands to grow from seeds of betrayal
and we cry again to You, Who sees it all,
What is left to pray?
No mighty words,
No joyous songs,
No unselfish pleas
spring from this broken humanity.

Father, can You help us be willing?
Willing to cast aside what we thought we knew...
Willing to be quiet and give You time...
Willing to hear, and to follow Your voice again,
though Your words, Your wisdom and Your ways
are not those of this world...
Willing to arise, to change direction, to march again...
Willing to walk a path veiled in clouds
where Your light shines only upon the next step...
Willing to share, unashamed, the words of Your Spirit...
Willing to ransom all, for the sake of eternal Truth...
Willing to listen, learn and remember
That in the middle of the hurricane
You're still speaking to Your children
in whispers.

❧

"The Lion's Gate" Jerusalem   *Becky McCarthy*

146

The Courtyard

I hadn't been to the city in over a month. It was my least favorite place to be, and I steeled myself as I walked through the gate into the crowded, bustling marketplace.

My youngest son had been gravely ill for many months and I'd made the long trip that day in hopes of bartering for some meat and vegetables. I'd spent everything I had on medicines, but nothing had helped. Now the physicians were saying the sickness had done permanent damage and that my little boy would not live much longer. I refused to believe them and prayed that some nourishing soup with healing herbs might bring him strength.

I passed the vendors with their cages of doves and felt a twinge of guilt. Others were buying them to offer as sacrifices at the temple, but I had neither the time nor the money. I hadn't been very consistent about keeping the laws lately, and the priests wouldn't approve of this further omission. Ducking my head, I hurried past the wealthy Pharisees gathered on the temple steps. Fortunately, they were deep in a heated discussion and uninterested in a common woman like me. I hoped not to run into anyone I knew. Regardless of how well-intentioned people might be, I didn't have the emotional energy to answer questions about my son's condition.

The atmosphere in the market felt different than usual. People seemed agitated and distracted and I overheard snatches of conversations and debates about prisoners and Pilot's decision to release one of them in honor of Passover. I'd completely forgotten about the holiday! No wonder there were so many people in town.

Religion and politics – I had little interest in either. My focus was on providing for my children. I was thankful that God had given me skillful hands so that I could create goods to sell in the city – but I had nothing in common with these folks. My wealth was not that of the women I saw here, draped in fine fabrics and gold, whose maidservants carried their purchases. My treasures were my children, and I counted my fortune not in coins but in the blessings of love we shared. I hated having to leave them home alone, and today, the only thing on my mind was to transact my business quickly so that I could get back.

147

I was about to offer one of my lamb's wool shawls to a vendor who'd purchased them in the past, when a loud ruckus erupted further down the street. Driven by curiosity, a sea of shoppers immediately headed in that direction and I was swept involuntarily along with them. The government buildings were just around the corner and when they came into view I could see that the noise was coming from an angry mob in the courtyard. Soldiers were shoving people back and tempers were flaring. It looked like a trial had just let out and I wondered what notorious criminal would provoke such a scene.

Just as I reached the outskirts of the crowd, the soldiers succeeded in parting it, and I saw a man being drug toward the whipping post. My stomach reeled. I had never been able to understand how people could bear to watch such brutality as was done there. It frightened me to think that the same people who flocked to see bloodshed and violence were my neighbors. That was one of the main reasons I'd moved to the country. We lived very humbly, but my children were safe, and life was peaceful there.

As I turned to leave, I heard a woman cry out. The desperate sound was between a scream and a wail, and it cut through all the other voices. *"Jesus! My Lord! No! No! Don't do this to him! He's innocent!"*

I spotted the woman and recognized her. She was a well-known prostitute who made her living in the marketplace, but I hadn't seen her on the streets for a long time. The man standing next to her spit in her face and yelled, *"Shut up, you whore! This guy's getting what he deserves! He thinks he's some kind of a messiah and he's been going around stirring up trouble in the whole region! A good thrashing will bring him back down to earth! King of the Jews? What a joke! He isn't* **my** *king!* **Crucify him!"**

Jesus? This couldn't be the same Jesus I knew of. He was a teacher and miracle worker whose message was one of peace and love. I'd seen and heard him myself.

The prostitute's screams continued while other angry voices echoed what the man had shouted at her. It all clashed like a sickening chord that struck and reverberated ominously through the chambers of my heart. Something was very wrong.

—— ◆ ——

148

ᘗy mind went back to the day a friend had told me that a healer by the name of Jesus, was in our region. My heart leapt at the hope of receiving a miracle for my little son, and I immediately made plans for us to travel to the seashore where he was teaching.

We left home the next morning at daybreak and made it to the coast by late morning, where we found a large, eager audience already gathered. Jesus arrived without any fanfare and began telling parables that we all – men and women, boys and girls, young and old – could understand. His words brought life and hope.

The time flew by. We hadn't expected to be there so long, and the children, along with a lot of other people, were getting hungry. No one wanted to leave, but I had almost decided we would have to when we heard someone shout that the men who'd come with Jesus were distributing food. As encouraging as that was to hear, we were so far toward the back that it seemed unlikely there would be any left for us.

Then, loud exclamations of excitement drew our attention. I stood on tiptoe and could see baskets of food being passed through the crowd. With every person served, the cheers grew louder, and when the baskets finally made it to the family next to us we saw what all the commotion was about. With each piece of bread and fish they took, more appeared in its place! When we reached in for our own portions, we witnessed this miracle ourselves. It was impossible, yet it happened before our eyes.

After every person at the gathering had been fed, there was still plenty of food left over. And, while all of this was going on, Jesus was sitting on a little knoll, sharing lunch with a small group of children, and smiling from ear to ear.

——— ♦ ———

ᚦhis man in the courtyard couldn't possibly be the one whom I'd seen bless so many, but I had to know for sure. I edged my way through the agitated throng until I could get a closer look.

Horror gripped my heart when I recognized the beaten, bloodied face of the healer whose beautiful smile was etched on my memory. The soldiers had tied his hands to the post and torn the robe from his back. I could not bear to watch what I knew was coming, and my instinct was to

149

run, but I was shaking so badly that my knees gave out. I crumbled, and within seconds, the crush of bodies trapped me in a nightmare where the cries and pleas of the prostitute became my own.

A burly centurion raised a hideous-looking whip studded with sharpened shards of metal and stone – the kind designed to slice through skin, leaving the muscle and nerves exposed. Depending upon the mood of the soldiers, these beatings were so brutal that prisoners often did not survive them.

For one deadly moment, the mob held its breath. Then, the first blow fell. Agonizing wails and vicious cheers mingled in a raucous roar as Jesus' body arched in pain. Scarlet stripes appeared where his flesh had been ripped open, and widened as every lash of the whip cut deeper to the bone. Blood oozed from the lacerations, flowed down his back and soaked his robe.

The soldier was thorough, and the scourging did not end until Jesus' body no longer moved. Most of the spectators seemed satisfied and the crowd quickly disbursed. The morbid show was over and they headed back home, to the marketplace, the temple, or to whatever it was they'd been doing before the uproar began. Others stood rooted to the ground in numb shock. The prostitute had incurred the wrath of those around her, and lay face down, her body heaving with sobs. We pitiful few who remained were no threat to the soldiers. They cut the cords and left Jesus' limp body to fall, then gathered in a circle a short distance away. I didn't stop to consider what they might do to me if they saw me run to him.

Falling to my knees, I pulled the shawl from my bag and laid it gently over the gruesome wounds on his back. When he did not move, I feared he was unconscious or worse.

"Teacher?" I whispered.

His hair was matted with blood and sweat, and I reached out to move the strands from his forehead. In the instant that I touched him, the courtyard and the evil surrounding us ceased to exist…for the windows of Heaven opened, and I looked into the eyes of God. Ancient and wise, filled with incomprehensible love and pain – they were not eyes of this world. He seemed to recognize me, but I didn't know how that could be possible. Though I'd tried for hours, I'd never been able to get close to him that day at the shore.

——— ♦ ———

After the supernatural provision of food, everyone pressed forward to ask for his blessing, and it wasn't long before reports of more miracles began to travel through the crowd. Upon hearing them, I held my children tighter and tried desperately to reach Jesus. I watched, and wept tears of joy along with the other mothers whose children he cured, and before long, the hope I'd held for my little boy's healing blossomed into unshakeable faith. Jesus was helping everyone who came to him, and I knew he would do the same for us.

But word of the events had spread quickly to the surrounding villages, and more people were arriving by the minute. We waited all afternoon, and the lines seemed never to grow shorter. The sun was setting, and the road was unsafe at night for women and children alone. Finally, to our great disappointment, we had to leave.

We went to bed that night still filled with the wonder of all we'd seen and heard. Every evening since then, I'd retold Jesus' stories to the children, and they always begged to hear *"...just one more, Mama..."* until they finally fell asleep.

———— ♦ ————

I'd heard, since then, that many people believed Jesus was the promised Messiah sent by God. Those in power had obviously gotten wind of that, and were threatened. Now, an innocent man lay bleeding in this courtyard, and far worse was to come. I did not want to be part of a world where such evil injustice could befall one who had done nothing but good.

His eyes remained locked on mine, and suddenly, though I cannot explain how, I knew he'd heard my thoughts. I was utterly helpless to relieve his suffering, and in agony, I could only moan, *"Oh, my Lord...my Lord..."*

His swollen lips parted slightly and I leaned close to hear his words, but before he could speak, a rough hand grabbed my shoulder. A soldier shoved me aside and they drug Jesus away. I never saw him again.

———— ♦ ————

Another generation has been born since that day. My children are grown now with families of their own, and have blessed me with grandchildren who are a constant source of joy. When their parents bring them to visit, the little ones beg me to tell them stories of the Great Teacher who loved children and worked mighty miracles. They know all of the stories by heart, but still listen as intently as though each time were the first. Their eyes grow sad when I tell them how He suffered, but sparkle again when I remind them that He is so mighty that not even death could hold Him, and that He came back to life, and reigns as King of Heaven and Earth for all eternity.

They know that even though He is in charge of the entire universe, He loves each one of them so much that He will always come when they need His Help, for He is never further than a prayer away.

"When I was a young mother, and your parents were still children of your age, I needed to make a trip to the city one day. Zachariah was the oldest, and very protective of his younger sister and brother, so although I never liked having to leave, I knew I could trust his judgment when I had to be away.

As you know, it's a long way to Jerusalem, and it was late by the time I returned. The day had been a very sad one for me, but something wonderful had happened to the children while I was gone and they'd been waiting anxiously for my return. When they saw me coming, they ran down the road to meet me, and I ran to meet them, too. The burden of my sorrows fell away when I hugged them close – and they were so excited that they were all talking at the same time.

"Mama, Mama! A man came to the house! He was shining so bright that we thought he must be an angel from Heaven! He knew our names, and was so kind! He asked us if we'd had lunch and when we said we hadn't, he said he had extra food and was happy to share. We sat outside, and while we were eating he told us he'd seen you in the city and that you would be home soon. He told us a wonderful story and then he said it was our turn to tell him one, so we told him about the day at the seashore when we saw the bread and fish appear before our eyes! He laughed and said he knew all about that event and was glad we'd had a chance to be a part of it.

Then, he said he'd heard our little brother was sick. Sarah started to cry, but he told her not to be sad, and he asked if we would take him to where Daniel was sleeping. When we did, he knelt beside the bed and drew a sign on Daniel's forehead with his fingertip, and then Daniel woke up! Mama, you wouldn't have believed it! He smiled at the man and hugged him, and then he jumped up out of the bed and ran all around the house looking for you! We ran after him, and then, when we looked for the man again, he was gone! We even looked down the road, but he had disappeared!"

"So, can you guess, my precious ones, who ran into my arms *first* on the road that day? And can you imagine how I felt when I saw him running as fast as his little legs would carry him, holding his arms out, laughing and shouting, *"Mamma! Mamma! Look at me! I can run! I'm all better now!"*

"That's when one little voice always cries out proudly, *'That was my Papa, wasn't it Grandma?! Jesus healed my Papa!'* Then they all tease me about my tears, for they know that's what happens when their Grandmother's cup overflows with joy.

"He is despised and rejected by men;
A man of sorrows and acquainted with grief.
We hid our faces from him...and esteemed him not.
Surely He is the One who has borne our grief
and carried our sorrows.
He was wounded for our transgressions,
He was bruised for our iniquities,
the chastisement of our peace was laid upon Him
And with His stripes we are healed."

The Prophet Isaiah

S.G.Rose

HANDS

With each day of this painful trial
that slips away into Your hands,
the morning fog lifts just a little bit earlier
and I can more clearly see You.

You have not shared Your plan with me,
but I can count the blessings that have gone before.
Salvaged, like jewels,
from the destruction that surrounds me.

Your promise is to heal, and
I have seen You touch and restore, before.
You *have*. You *do*. You *will*.
I believe!

Father, though my baby is suffering now
You gave Your own precious Boy
and I am sure that your future sight did not ease Your pain
as He bled at His enemies' hands.

You watched the whip strike every blow
and felt the nails as they pierced His sinless flesh,
and You've stood here beside me, too,
while my innocent child suffers
at the hands of those who practice and fail.

Where is the healing we seek from this world?
You guide men with knowledge,
yet the answers escape,
and they walk away shaking their heads.
The wise turn again with open hands,
for healing comes *always* from You.

Just as the days had to be fulfilled
· when Your Son stood His test,
so Your will must prevail here, now,
in our small corner of time –
my little boy's and mine.
For though this mother's life I've laid down
begging to take his place, his pain,
he is Your child, first.

He is safest in the Hands that gave his soul life,
and I can only trust and wait,
for Your days and Your ways are not mine,
and You,
Father of us all,
love him even more than I.

The Tomb

My illness was terminal. The doctors had given up and there was nothing left to do but fill the grim days with distractions and charades of normality. I told my family not to worry about me – that I'd made my peace and was resigned to my fate – but in the loneliness of night, tears poured from my frightened soul.

I grew weaker, until each painful breath felt like it might be my last. A close friend of ours was a healer, but he'd been traveling for some time, and was unaware of my condition. My sisters had been trying desperately to locate him, and had just received the encouraging news that he was in a region just a couple days' journey away. They immediately sent a courier with an urgent letter, and we all relaxed a little, knowing that he would hasten to my aid. Regardless of what the doctors said, we had faith in his ability to cure me.

A week passed, and word returned that our message had been delivered. We watched and waited for several more days, but when there was no sign of our friend, my sisters became increasingly worried and upset. I overheard one of the neighbors say that even if he was on his way, it was doubtful I could last that long. They didn't know it, but I heard their hushed conversations, and listened to their last hopes die. Their premature grief heralded my inevitable end, and I was helpless against all of it.

Though the faithful stood watch at my door, Death slipped past them that night. I fought valiantly, but victory was his as he ground out the last spark of my life with his heel. Then, he laughed and proclaimed himself undefeated. I hadn't been much of a challenge, he crowed, but no human ever was, which made it easy for him to hold on to his title. A worthy adversary might make his job more interesting, but none had ever stepped forward.

They sealed my remains in the family tomb. My sisters and the mourners wept for the loss of my life. They wept because they had not been able to save me, and they wept because the one who could have done so had not bothered to come.

None of it mattered to me. The place where my soul had once shone had been swallowed by a desolate void. I was now no more than a memory in the hearts of those still living, who I hoped would choose to remember only the good.

Death's darkness was deeper than I'd imagined. In the icy silence I slept, and dreamed that I was not in the tomb but that the tomb was in me. A familiar voice called my name in the dream from somewhere far away. It grew louder, closer, more insistent. And then he appeared – Jesus, my belated, beloved friend! He smiled, raised his hand in greeting, and light shattered the blackness into a million pieces.

I awoke and jumped up, but he was gone.

Then, I heard the grating sound of the stone being rolled away from the entrance to my tomb. Sunlight streamed in and the crisp air filled my lungs. Jesus shouted at me to come out and he didn't have to ask twice. I'd never felt better, but that wasn't the case for many of the spectators, who either fainted or ran away terrified at the sight of me dragging my burial shroud.

𝕯eath met his match that day when the Son of God snatched me from his grasp. I never feared meeting the Reaper again, and by the time I did, the rules had changed. Jesus had become the undisputed champion, and although Death refused to retire, he had been stripped of all his power and was a mere shell of his former arrogant self.

I left the planet about two thousand years ago, but the last time I checked, you still had the advantage down there. I wonder if you all know how fortunate you are.

You see, I can still remember those four days in that tomb.

"I am the resurrection and the life.
He who believes in me, though he were dead, yet shall he live.
And whoever lives and believes in me shall never die."
•
Jesus

The Story of Lazarus
•
John, Chapter 11

Miracles

When all the tears have been cried

And all expectations have gone unmet

When the desperate thrashing has stopped

And hopes and dreams lie shattered

When all our ways have failed

And the chorus of voices has grown silent

When prayers have emptied our soul

In the death of emotions spent

When we've surrendered, in humble, broken acceptance

When holding on has become impossible

And everything dear has slipped through our clutching fingers

When we've let it all go

Lost it all

And the trivial matters no more

When faith's last breath can be seen

Only by One far greater than ourselves

He walks quietly in

Unhindered

And miracles happen.

✦

S.G.Rose

From the Maze...

If I were free, I'd change this dark sky
Fly to the sun, stop wondering why
Leave choices and questions, let time take my tears
Run with new purpose, stop counting the years
'Til I'm free.

Deeds and decisions, plans and promises made
The past turns to dust each skillful charade
I thought I knew then, and I think I know now
But each day reveals that I'm still learning how
To be free.

We grope through this maze, taught by every dead end
Mapping out our own ways, starting over again
Turn the next corner, will it be the one
Where rays of hope shine on the pathway Home
Where we're free.

When I first entered here, signs were easy to see
But I leaned on the shoulder of humanity
Walls hide the truth, need makes us weak
Lost, running in circles, we reach, we bleed
And forget that we should be free.

Passion's vows of this flesh will meet crossroads of fate
We must each walk alone through Eternity's gate
Where One higher looks on and understands why
We stumble and falter, and hears our cry
To be free.

If You will just call to me, I'll hear the sound
And follow it out, my true path found
I'll emerge into light and Your arms of love
Then at last I will know what You saw from above
When I'm free.

161

S.G.Rose

Resurrection

*"Eye has not seen, nor ear heard, neither have entered into the heart of man,
those things which God has prepared for them that love Him..
But God has revealed them unto us by His Spirit:
for the Spirit searches all things ~ yes, the deep things of God."*

•

II Corinthians 2:9-10

What is praise and worship of God? People answer that question in many different ways. For me, it's acknowledging and reverencing His greatness, pouring out my love for Him, thanking Him for His mercy and blessings, rejoicing that I am His child, and opening my heart and mind to the fresh infilling of His Holy Spirit.

What many people don't realize is that there is also unlimited power in praise.

There was a lot I didn't know when I first yearned to find the perfect "house of worship" – a place where I would fit in with others like myself and where the person at the pulpit was truly God's choice for the job. Each group orchestrates and is characterized by its own version of worship, and anyone accustomed to expressing praise differently is likely to feel uncomfortable in the midst of those with a dissimilar form. If the congregation is singing solemn ancient hymns, and you shout praises and dance in the aisle, ushers will probably escort you out. If they're dancing in the aisles and you're sitting with your hands folded and a hymnal in your lap, they'll notice and be rightly concerned. All these unspoken shalts and shalt-nots get confusing, and *"God is not the author of confusion."* • I Corinthians 14:33

While we're wondering what's proper, or what we sound or look like, our attention is not on pure worship of God, but on protocol and the approval of men. If we settle for being led through pre-written texts or reciting words that were not born in our own hearts, then what's the point? It's supposed to be spontaneous *worship*, not a performance!

"...and when you are praying, don't use meaningless repetitions as the heathen do, for they think they will be heard for their much-speaking." • Jesus, Matthew 6:7

163

I'm fairly certain that God appreciates sincere praise in many forms, and I, personally am a strong advocate of freedom in worship. But it's also important to remember that if our expression is a distraction in a group that is worshipping differently, then love – as demonstrated by restraint – should prevail. • I Corinthians 14

A friend of mine was once asked to join her family at a church she described as *"dead."* She suffered through the solemn service and during the prayer, lamented to God that she ached to praise Him as freely as she usually did. To her surprise, He didn't sympathize.

*"My daughter, you have an inner woman. Let **her** sing and dance!"*

And so it was that during those early days of my spiritual growth, this subject often presented a real dilemma. One Sunday morning, I sat down in the front row of a church I was visiting more out of determination than desire. I sighed, opened the bulletin, and mumbled to myself, *"Okay, let's see what the rules are here. Ah, yes...the 'Order of Service.'"* I briefly pondered the definition of the word "Order," and read on. I wondered what the allotted minutes for the first sub-heading of *"Worship and Praise"* would hold, and expected they would probably be characteristically brief, while announcements, offerings, and the sermon took up the biggest part of the hour and ten minutes.

Would I know the songs? Would I be able to relax and have time to focus my heart on God, or would I be led, told what to recite, or hurried through that precious time? I'd heard so many different kinds of "worship and praise" that I wondered what really touched God. It seemed to me that for praise and worship to be pure, the worshipper should be filled with sincere emotions, but a lot of people seemed reluctant to exhibit those. To have to refrain from expressing less than what I felt, was dispiriting and stifling. If worship wasn't passionate adoration, then what was it?

We stood on cue and the singing began. I followed the words projected on the overhead screen, found my alto part, lifted my hands to a conservative height, and joined in, but after the first few measures, I was overcome by such a deep weariness and feeling of futility that I couldn't squeeze out another note. I shut my mouth, closed my eyes, and cried out to Jesus in my heart, while the congregation sang on.

"Lord! What's wrong with me? I want to praise You, but I don't know how anymore! In the beginning I thought I did, but every church

*thinks differently. Please, Lord, show me how to worship the way **You** want me to!"*

With the last word of my plea, something extraordinary happened. While I remained fully in touch with my physical body, below, another part of my being was simultaneously lifted up and out of it to a vantage point near the ceiling above and to the left of the pulpit, where I could look out over the entire room.

From that higher perspective, I saw that a miraculous change had come over the congregation. Whereas every seat had been full when the singing began, only a third of the people now remained standing, and they had been transformed into the most beautiful beings imaginable. As I stared in awe, I was given the knowledge that that these were our *glorified* bodies, and that we – for I could see myself amongst them – were not flesh and bone, but pure *spirit*.

Although we retained our individuality, we shared a similar appearance, and as we sang and moved in consummate unity and harmony, we did so with the same singular purpose of mind and heart. We were, quite literally, *"one in the Spirit."*

I took in every glorious attribute of the saints, for my heart knew us to be that. Oh, how I wish I could adequately convey what I was shown, and somehow paint a living picture for you! I have tried in so many ways to do so, often with more numerous and illustrious adjectives than I ultimately decided upon here. Such beauty simply does not exist on earth, and no matter how hard I try, all of my descriptions will always fall far short. In the end, I must trust the Holy Spirit to illuminate for you what I, with human words, cannot.

We worshippers were dressed in long sleeved, floor-length robes made of light. The fibers from which the cloth was woven were themselves alive, and the iridescent, golden-white fabric cascaded weightlessly from the neckline and sleeves down to the floor in soft, shimmering folds. While I was observing this from above, I could simultaneously *feel* the fabric moving as a part of my body, below.

Our skin was flawless as the finest porcelain and smooth as rose petals. Our hair was the texture of spun gold and fell in thick, silken waves to our shoulders with not a single strand out of place. Foreheads, noses, cheekbones and jaw lines were the work of a master sculptor, and crystal-clear blue eyes were fixed on something yet unseen to me from my position above.

As I stared, enthralled, at these shining beings who moments earlier had appeared to my eyes as ordinary people, the knowledge was imparted to me that I was looking upon the *Masterpieces of Creation.*

My attention was then guided back to an awareness of my own changed body. Human flesh cannot know such perfection, even at the peak of health and fitness, for it exists only in a place void of physical, mental and spiritual pollution – a world of absolute holiness.

I could feel every organ inside my body performing its own distinct function – and as they operated in consummate harmony, I understood, and was in awe of how precious and vital even the smallest connections and workings of every cell were to the whole.

Each breath I took filled perfect lungs with sweet, pure air and a tingling flow of energy circulated through my veins. Like a current of millions of super-charged particles of light, it was the most rejuvenating, exhilarating sensation imaginable, and I knew that it was to that glorified body, as blood is to the human body. In the same way that our earthly bodies feel warmth, cold, hunger and other sensations, it was the nature of the glorified body to feel this energy flow. As it traveled through each cell, it fed and infused them with life. It contained everything needed to sustain that existence.

A great sense of anticipation permeated the room, and I knew something tremendous was about to happen. Suddenly, in the place where the altar had stood, a vortex opened and brilliant white light blazed forth. It was so intense that it obscured the form of the One at its center, but we all knew that Christ had come to join us.

The light was the pure, undiluted holiness of perfect Love. Human eyes would have been blinded by it, but to our glorified bodies, it was life. It poured over and through us and we absorbed it. It flowed into every corner of the room, and I was caused to notice that it cast no shadows. Those who were standing in the back of the room received as much light as those in the front.

I was then shown the distinct energy particles within the light, and was given the revelation that the light shining from Christ, and the energy I could feel flowing through my veins, *were the same substance.*

We stood facing the light, our arms stretched upward in ecstatic communion, our eyes, our souls, our entire beings welcoming and

166

surrendering to its glory. We were one with it and it with us. I felt it pour into my fingertips and course through my body. It completed the cycle and then poured out again through my hands and back to Christ, its Source.

I was taking part in a never-ending exchange of love between the Creator and His children – the ultimate union of God and man. It was absolute fulfillment, indescribable bliss, and there was nothing greater beyond it – nor did there need to be. I did not want it to end. This was who we were created to be and this is what we were created to do! I'd been transformed and I didn't want to come back down to earth. This fusion with the Light was my true existence, and anything less would feel like death. I could remember how dull and painful my human body felt by comparison and the thought of going back to it was abhorrent.

(Note: One other particular part of this vision has always been difficult for me to share. Should this be the constraint of the Holy Spirit, I have not included it in this account. I will only say that anything suffered in this lifetime is utterly insignificant and forgotten when we are changed. • *John 15:20; Colossians 1:24; 2 Timothy 2:12 - 3:12; I Peter 4:12-13 - 5:10.)*

The entire experience lasted only minutes, but I was so immersed in the spiritual and physical sensations of that higher reality that I didn't notice when the organ music stopped and the singing ended. While everyone else sat down, I remained standing there in the front row, with my arms still stretched upward into the light. Then, I felt a nudge at my elbow and heard the whispered words, *"It's time to sit down."*

Abruptly, I was back in the real world, in an ordinary room with an ordinary pulpit, surrounded by ordinary folks who were staring at me curiously. It was a harsh, disorienting return.

I sat down, but could not focus on the pastor's words. Light still filled my mind and I could feel the energy particles tingling inside. I wanted desperately to hold on to them for as long as I could, and I squeezed my eyes shut, sat very still and prayed fervently to be taken back to that other state of existence. But as hard as I tried to retain it, the vital spiritual energy began to fade, and I realized that my human body could not recognize, absorb, process or contain it nor more than a sieve can hold water. I could actually *feel* the light particles leaking out of my cells.

I tried desperately to reconnect, but could no longer distinguish the inner workings of my body. I could only sit with my hands resting on my lap, palms up, and watch helplessly as the last bits of dancing light left my fingertips.

Then, I cried. I had never before expected to feel my own life force, but now it seemed wrong and absurd that I couldn't – like being cheated out of a birthright. Now, every breath felt thick and heavy and the blood moved like sludge through my veins. This was the human body I had always known, and compared to the other one, it was a miserable, depressing liability.

Sadness overwhelmed me. I wanted that other body back! And I wanted to be with my Lord that way, forever! Why, when such ecstasy was possible, did we have to live deprived of it? Could it be achieved here? The voice that had been guiding me through the experience answered, *"Only in part."* and gently explained that the other existence was the form our souls would take when we had overcome this world, shed our human flesh and left all earthly burdens behind.

For the rest of the service I sat with my head bowed, staring at the hands that had tingled with holy energy. I replayed every detail of the experience over and over. Why had I been given this taste of such bliss? I would never feel the same about this arduous human lifetime again! Beyond the revelation of the glory to come, was there something more I was supposed to understand?

The closing song of the service was announced and we stood to our feet. It was a well-known hymn, but before I could form the first word, my Lord's voice echoed within my soul:

"Now, do you know how to worship?"

"...the hour is coming, and now is, when the true worshippers shall worship the Father in spirit and in truth: For the Father seeks such to worship Him. God is a Spirit: and they that worship Him must worship Him in spirit and in truth."

Jesus, John 4:23-24

Invitation

My children sit dutifully in stiff rows
At the scheduled time in a place they call My House.
Gathered here, they assume I am home
Though most do not greet Me.

Called to order, the meeting begins
With the chanting of sacred hymns.
The music is grand ~ four part harmony
With all of the proper accompaniment.
Whose ears is it for
If theirs do not hear Me when I join in their song?

I would speak eternal mysteries to them
But they desire the teachings of men.
I long to heal their suffering
But they do not feel My touch.

I reach to embrace them with the deepest love
But they do not run to Me.
I have strength to give them
But they seem to have no need of it.

I long to show them My face
But they turn their eyes away.
I would be their champion and give them certain victory
But they do not listen for the trumpet.

I could shelter them from harm beneath My wings
But they scurry away

When their service is over
Back out into their world.

I long to take them to where I am
But they do not yet know Me
Or why I have come.

❧

"These people draw nigh unto Me with their mouths
and honor Me with their lips,
but their hearts are far from Me.
In vain they worship Me,
teaching for doctrines
the commandments of men."
•
Matthew 15:8-9

170

The Potter's Cup

I would rather be
A humble vessel
Fashioned and fired
By my Master's hand,
Comfortably chipped and worn
From everyday use by Him,
Waiting at His table
To be emptied and filled again,
Overflowing with living water,
Taken to the street,
And poured out freely
To beggars
Who thirst for truth...

*T*han a fragile
Be-jeweled collector's piece,
Kept from hard use,
Hidden behind stained glass doors
In the house of the rich,
Taken out only
On sacred, scheduled occasions,
And passed around
To refined persons, who,
Cloaked in ceremonial superiority,
Sip through tight lips,
The watered down Word.

♦

"...To everything there is a Season"...

...and a time for every purpose under Heaven.
God has made everything beautiful in its own time, but
although He has planted eternity in our hearts...we cannot
see the whole scope of God's work from beginning to end."

•

Ecclesiastes 3

172

The Legend of The Great Fisherman

Summer held the countryside in her warm embrace like a nurturing mother who'd been away from her children too long. In the fresh morning hours they were allowed their play, but come afternoon, she would spread her patchwork comforter out over the landscape and sweetly lull all but the meadow's most industrious inhabitants into a drowsy state of slow motion beneath it.

Contented sighs from Heaven caressed the rolling hills and the hot air hummed with the sounds of the insects assigned to the thistles and foxgloves. Except for an occasional staccato squabble between the crows perched in the old oak trees, nothing marred the idyllic scene. At the end of the lane a white birch forest stood watch over a pond. It's welcome shade and cooling breezes had been calling to the familiar figure who was on his way there.

The man's sandals kicked up small clouds of dust and the crickets fell silent as he passed by. Like the rest of the countryside's residents, he was not in a hurry, and stopped now and then to inhale the fragrance of a wildflower or to follow the flight of a hawk circling lazily above. Slung over his shoulder was an old, worn fisherman's net that swung softly from side to side as he made his way down the well-traveled path.

At the pond, the weeping willows draped themselves over the shallows, devotedly sheltering the unseen creatures below. The afternoon was slipping away, and the young rainbow trout were awakening from their naps, hungry. In search of snacks, they darted back and forth just under the water's surface, gobbling what they could find, and daring one another to hurtle up into the world above to capture wayward bugs. With total abandon, the young fish gave themselves over to the joy of living, which could be risky business in the pond. Like all young things, they expected their energy and speed to last forever. They paid little attention to the warnings of their elders, and were bored by the lectures and stories of the Old One, the pond's resident living legend.

The ancient trout's reputation preceded him. He'd survived the harshest winters on record and had outwitted every fisherman ever to come to the pond. His extensive repertoire of stories gained him new respect each time he retold them – or so he liked to think. He had outlived most of his friends and family, and except for an occasional visit to the busy waters above, he stayed holed up in the dark seclusion of the depths – in smug, if lonely, safety.

It happened, on this day, that the old fish had decided to warm himself in the sun-dappled shallows near the place where the young trout frolicked. A wooden bridge connected the meadow to the birch tree forest on the other side of the pond, and he had a favorite spot below it. From there, he could keep a vigilant eye on all the action.

He loved the placid green waters of his home, and had fought long and hard to remain in them. Now and then, when the mood struck, he'd express his quiet thanks to the One he instinctively knew had created all the beauty that lay above and within his shimmering liquid world. Once, he'd even thought he heard the Creator answer, but that had been long ago and he now dismissed the incident as the overactive imagination of youth. A hard life had made him fiercely practical, and had taught him that the only one he could count on was himself. He didn't believe in the literal companionship of Deity, nor did he expect to receive any communication, help, or comfort from some unseen force. That sort of need was clearly an indication of weakness and spawned other unhealthy dependencies that he could live fine without. And if further justification was necessary, his own personal experience with so-called love had convinced him that it was a dangerous emotion that left its victims confused and vulnerable – not to mention betrayed, wounded and abandoned.

"Trust no one but yourself!" he repeatedly admonished the other fish. *"I am living proof that only those who fend for themselves survive, and I have my own strength, speed, common sense and determination to thank for the fact that I am still alive and able to tell about it!"*

174

And tell about it he did, with continual warnings to all who would listen, about the snares, dangers and deceptions they must learn to overcome, followed by sour predictions of the gruesome fates sure to befall them if they refused to take his advice. The Old One had little energy to do much else these days other than observe, judge and lecture those who shared his kingdom – and this day was no exception.

He settled down into a spot between two moss-covered rocks. A few trout spotted him and immediately swam in too close for his comfort. Feigning annoyance, he sent a cloud of sand swirling around them with one swish of his ragged, yet still powerful tail, and they immediately backed off to a more respectful distance. After the waters had cleared, he addressed his small audience, who listened solemnly as he retold the stories of his adventures and narrow escapes from the predators and fishermen who had sought to capture him over the years.

"Don't be naive!" he warned them. *"They are all the same – the men who come here to our pond with their lures and bait. Those seemingly harmless disguises hide deadly hooks that will find their way into your jaw if you are stupid enough to fall for such enticements! Once hooked, you will be reeled in with no hope of escape!*

Did I ever tell you about the time that…Oh, I did? Well then, you know how that story ends! Just remember that none of those who met this fate have ever returned to tell us what lies beyond. We only know that they have been taken away from our midst forever.

Beware! *Hunger and temptation can dull your judgment, and these men will prey upon your innocence and your need. My advice is that you greatly fear any man who stands upon the bridge. Keep your distance – do you hear me? Go hungry, if you must! I am telling you from experience – **no** fisherman can be trusted!"*

At that very same instant, the Old One's ominous words were punctuated by the creaking of the boards on the bridge. His pupils scattered and hid under the nearby lily pads, where they knew to wait until he gave the signal that danger had passed.

All was still, but strangely, instead of the dread that commonly descended at the presence of man, peace settled over the waters. The younger trout sensed it, and one by one they began to slip out into the open – their curiosity drawing them nearer and nearer to the bridge.

"Fools!" the Old One groaned, as he lodged himself more firmly down between the rocks. All of his senses – honed razor-sharp from years of mistrust – were keenly on edge as he waited for the inevitable

hook. But it did not come. No lure snapped above the surface and no bait plopped beneath.

No one but fishermen came to the pond, and many were regulars. Their styles gave them away, and the Old One was able to evade them all. His survival depended upon maintaining his advantage. Who was up there, and what did they want?

Suddenly, as if plucked from the misty archives of his memory by an unseen hand, a vivid image appeared in the Old One's mind. A day much like this one...a certain feeling...a voice...

His musings were interrupted by a sound from above. He brushed the reverie aside and snapped to attention, ready to dive into the depths at the first sign of danger.

"Fisherman..."

It was probably just the breeze moving through the cattails or the willow branches brushing across the pond's surface.

"Fisherman...We are with you."

No...there it was again...someone speaking. He'd only heard the fisherman's footsteps, so who was *"We?"*

The voice was hauntingly familiar, and again, memories crowded to the front of his mind. Was it the same voice he'd heard upon the Wind when he was young? Unlikely. That had been his imagination – and he must be imagining this, too. Perhaps sleep had overtaken him as it often did these days and he was dreaming. That would explain it. He blinked his eyes and shook himself, but when he looked around, he saw by the reactions of some of the other fish that they had heard something, too. So, his old ears *weren't* playing tricks on him!

The fisherman answered the voice of the Wind and a companionable conversation followed. The Old One felt awkward as he eavesdropped on the exchange. Words of love and commitment always made him uncomfortable. But these went deeper, and stirred within him a host of long-buried emotions that he'd been largely successful at ignoring...until now.

As softly as it had begun, the conversation above ended. The Wind's words faded to whispers barely distinguishable from the rustling of the leaves, and strain as he would, the Old One could hear no more. Then, the strands of a net broke the surface of the water. He eyed it suspiciously, backed off, and expected the others would follow his example – but to my amazement, fish shot out of the shadows from every direction and filled it to overflowing.

The fisherman laughed with joy, the trees clapped their hands, and the birds of the forest and meadow burst into song. Their melodies filled the sky as the fisherman slowly drew his net up from the water. Then, he quietly left the bridge.

Twilight descended upon the pond and its remaining residents were left to contemplate what they had witnessed. For many of them, sleep would not come easy that night, and when it did, their dreams would be perplexing. They would awaken the next morning and carry on with the necessary business of living, but the visit of the mysterious fisherman would not be forgotten.

◆

Summer lingered as long as she could, spending her last melancholy days ripening the golden ears of corn and plumping the juicy blackberries that hung in heavy clusters from the bushes bordering the lane. Before anyone was quite ready, Autumn breezed in with her usual fanfare, and nudged her sister sweetly aside. She was anxious to get on with the harvest, and soon, wagons overflowed with mountains of pumpkins and sheaves of grain stood like sentinels in rows that stretched as far as the eye could see across the fields.

At the pond, scarlet leaves fluttered down from the latticework canopy of vine maples onto the water's surface where they floated like hundreds of brightly-painted fairy tale gondolas. Left to the whim of the ripples, they drifted and swayed aimlessly, as though awaiting the boarding of miniature navigators who would steer them to shore.

Some time had passed since the visit of the mysterious fisherman, but hushed discussion still continued about what had really happened that day. The man's reputation had grown to legendary proportions, and now rivaled even that of the Old One. Although many fish had swum into his net, a fair number had not, and accounts of the event varied greatly amongst them. Interpretations of the words spoken by the Wind were many, and each different school of thought had its own following. What had taken place in the minds of those who had given themselves to the fisherman was a mystery. Popular theories were that they must have succumbed to powerful magic, hypnosis, or been otherwise seduced into the net. Why else would they abandon all common sense?

At the risk of ridicule, a few fish had reluctantly admitted that they had heard a voice call their names. But though the temptation had been strong, they had remembered the Old One's warnings. Obviously, he had been right, for while the others had acted impulsively and been taken, the smart ones had kept their wits about them and stayed put.

The general consensus amongst the non-superstitious was that eventually there would emerge a logical explanation for the strange occurrence of that day and other days like it. It challenged their present understanding, but given time and evolution, a clearer understanding of the natural world in which they lived would be revealed, and then there would be an end to this mass hysteria once and for all.

Leaving debates to the younger generation, the Old One made his home deeper in the pond than ever. He wasn't in the mood to swim to the surface or to conduct training classes for the younger trout. Upon his retreat, he'd made it clear that he wanted to be left alone, and some suspected he was not well. Those who knew him best were concerned. They shook their heads sadly when his name came up in conversation, for while it was true that he had lived many more seasons than any of them, everyone knew that even the smartest fish could not live forever.

◆

*W*inter was running quite late that year. Autumn had finished her work and was ready to rest. Her energy was waning, and she was beginning to wonder if he was ever going to show up. But just about the time she started to get downright cranky, he stole in one night and surprised her by trimming the pond with ice crystals that sparkled in the sun like the scattered strands of a diamond necklace. She forgave him his tardiness then, patted his whiskered face, and assured him that no one had really minded – which, except for her, was certainly true.

Later that same morning, the Old One was roused by a sunbeam that had made its way through the depths into his home. As the light poured down over him, it seemed to beckon him to swim up higher into the shallows to be touched by its warmth.

"Curious," he mused. *"The sun's never reached this far down before. Not even on the brightest summer day."*

Although he knew the seasons had changed, he'd not left his hiding place since the day of the fisherman. If any others had come to the bridge since then, he didn't know it, nor did he care.

The deepening chill in the waters signaled to him that food would soon become scarce and life harder to sustain. In his younger days, this would have kindled a heightened sense of self-preservation, savage determination and the invigorating challenge of survival against the odds, but he could no longer find those feelings, or any other motivation, within himself. He was weary. And today, like every other day, he just wanted to be left alone.

During the long, solitary months, the Old One had not been able to stop thinking about the words he'd heard spoken between the fisherman and the Wind. There was no longer any doubt in his mind. They had both called his name. In an effort to put an end to his confusion, he had finally abandoned his stern logic and had searched his memory for more details of that long-ago day in his youth when he thought he'd heard the Wind speak to him. There was no escaping the fact that the sounds and the sensations were the same. But on that first occasion, the Wind's words had come in response to his own prayer of thanks to the Creator for the beauty of his home. Did the Creator speak upon the Wind? And if so, why would they both betray him in such a manner as to send a fisherman, of all beings? Who *was* this man that these mighty forces should say to him *"We are with you?"*

All those who lived in the Pond knew they belonged to the Creator. They instinctively reverenced and obeyed Him, for the patterns of their lives had been shaped by His thoughts. The Wind was also part of their existence. Although they did not know where It came from or where It went, they knew It was all powerful and that It had no beginning nor end. The Wind simply *was*. It brought them signs and seasons, but It did not speak to them in words. Or so the Old One had believed until now.

That fisherman. Why did the Wind treat him so differently than the others? How would the Old One find out? And why did he feel this desperate need to know? What did any of it matter to him anyway? His instincts needled him daily with grim reminders of the inescapable fact that shortly, the seasons of his own life would come to an end. Just like the fading sun, he was doomed to become only a memory – a character in the stories others would tell.

What had become of the family and friends whose lives he'd shared in the past? Where were they now when he needed them? He thought about those who'd fallen victim to rod and reel, the few who had swum into the fisherman's net, and the others who had gone to sleep forever. The rest he seldom saw. They were around somewhere, he supposed, surviving on their own without his help. A pang of guilt told him he might be responsible for their absence. He knew he could be ornery, critical and sarcastic at times but it was just his way. They were too sensitive – needed to grow thicker scales. Instead of feeling hurt or taking offense, they should have considered how they might benefit from his appraisal of their personality flaws. But that never happened. Instead, they seemed even more determined to persist in their own ways. So, he'd given up on them. Empathy, tolerance and patience weren't his strong suits.

In any case, they were all gone, and there was no point in analyzing why. He'd meant well, done his best and this was just the way life had gone. *"Each creature for itself"* was his philosophy. He'd never been handed anything free in his life. He'd had to figure it all out on his own and earn it all himself, and he couldn't see where that had hurt him.

Yes, the Old One was quite satisfied with his beliefs. They had proven good enough to get him what he wanted, and more importantly, they'd kept him alive. But they were useless in the struggle to sort out this barrage of mixed feelings and memories, and provided no answers to the unsettling questions that that were surfacing from within the turmoil.

Isolated and alone, he was being forced to confront himself for the first time, and he had to admit that in spite of a lifetime of dependence upon no one else, he now felt the desperate need for something more. Maybe he'd overlooked or ignored it along the way. Perhaps it hadn't seemed important at the time. Whatever it was, its absence had been gnawing at him since he'd heard the voice call his name, and he'd vowed to himself that if he were to live long enough to hear that voice again, he would not hide nor flee – he would answer it. For he had to know – *must not die without knowing* – what more it might say to him.

Daydreams. It wasn't like him to waste time this way, and finding himself lost in them so often these days was disquieting. He shrugged off his musings, pulled himself together, and made a firm decision to channel his energy into more profitable activity. He would take this opportunity to follow the sunbeam up to the shallows instead, where he might find enough diversion to be of some small comfort. Perhaps watching the young fish at play would bring pleasant memories of happier days and crowd out these gloomy ones.

His heart was cheered a bit by the little pool of warmth the sun had created at his favorite spot. In a glance he observed that everything was much the same as it had been at the time of his last visit, allowing for the change in seasons and the increased activity essential to preparations for the cold months ahead.

His appearance caused a predictable stir among the other fish, and before long a continuous procession came to pay their respects. He expected them to request their favorite stories, but they were more interested in the reason for his retreat into seclusion. Their brazen curiosity was irritating. His short supply of patience was quickly depleted, and his curt, evasive answers sent the clear message that what he did or didn't do was none of their business. Insulted by his rebuff, the busybodies left him alone again as they hurried off to spread the gossip that it was indeed just as bad as had been rumored, if not worse: he was meaner than ever, looked terrible, and was obviously not well – not well at all.

The Old One bid them good riddance and ensconced himself down between the rocks. In the comfortable familiarity of that place, he succumbed, once again, to the temptation to let his mind wander over the most illustrious moments of his long, colorful life. They made for great stories, indeed. He'd never had trouble holding an audience in the old days. If the others didn't want to listen to him anymore, that was their loss.

He closed his eyes and one by one pinpointed, recreated and savored his greatest battles, triumphs, achievements and adventures. But in spite of the boost the well-chosen memories gave his sagging ego, an aggravating restlessness still plagued him. He watched the young trout swimming and playing together, and knew that they naturally shared something he had lost and could no longer feel. Inside, the persistent ache began again, and for once, instead of fighting it, he allowed the pain to swell until he could no longer choke back or deny the emotions that tore at his heart.

He, too, had once possessed the joy, love, trust and companionship that the young ones freely shared, and whether consciously or not, he had exchanged those irreplaceable treasures for cunning, power and pride. He could remember very few endearing, tender moments in his life that hadn't been overshadowed by his determination to remain independent, self-sufficient and in control. He'd gotten what he'd wanted and considered himself successful and wise, yet he now felt hopelessly weak and confused.

He was supposed to be the hero of this pond! They expected him to have all the answers, but if he had them, then why was his heart now breaking? What would they think if they knew how he really felt? He dreaded to believe that everything he'd so diligently preached over the years might lead the others to this same lonely, bewildered state of mind. What if he'd been wrong? It was all in question, now. Perhaps those who'd heard the voice and swam into the fisherman's net hadn't been misguided after all. Maybe they knew something he didn't.

"What an old fool I am," he muttered miserably, *"I can't even control myself anymore. I should have known that coming to the shallows would be a mistake."* Humiliated and angry with himself, yet determined to salvage what small amount of pride he had left, he decided to retreat to the depths, where he would hope – and wait – for a speedy, merciful death.

Before he could move, footsteps sounded upon the bridge. The last thing the Old One could bear to watch was the pitiful fate of another trout at the end of some fisherman's line, and he headed downward without looking back. What happened next, he scarcely dared believe, even though it had come in response to his deepest longing. As he swam back through the ray of sun that had guided him upward earlier, a great stillness penetrated the waters. Not a day had passed that he hadn't relived in his mind the sensations of that uncommon afternoon when the fisherman had called his name, and now, he was feeling them again.

The Old One sped back up toward the shallows where he could make out the figure on the bridge. The man was leaning over the railing, gazing down into the waters of the pond, and an old, worn net lay at his feet. After a moment, he sighed deeply and reluctantly took his eyes from the waters. Straightening up, he tilted his head backward, shaded his eyes with his hand, and looked into the sun. The old fish watched every move, determined to learn everything he could about the mysterious powers of persuasion that had drawn so many of his well-warned students into the fisherman's net.

The fellow's face was etched with wrinkles, but he wasn't old. Autumn's last sunny offering had prompted him to remove his shirt, revealing a well-muscled torso common to those who worked the land.

There didn't really seem to be anything out-of-the-ordinary about him – and then, the Old One saw the scars. Glistening jagged stripes crisscrossed the fisherman's shoulders and back, and there were others on his ribcage, hands and feet. The fish knew that such strength of build could be earned by laboring in the fields from seed time through harvest, but he had never seen such terrible scars. He bore his own collection proudly, of course – each like a medal of honor with a colorful story behind it – but they now seemed embarrassingly insignificant compared to whatever the fisherman had suffered. The Old One had to admit to a certain respect for the man's obvious endurance. He felt an unexpected comradery, but quickly cautioned himself to remain objective. He was only here to observe the man's tactics, and nothing more.

Then, the fisherman began to speak to the sky.

"Father Creator, for years beyond number I have come to this little pond. And many times those who heard Your words on the Wind have come to Me. This was their natural response for they had already grown to understand and trust in Our love as expressed here within their earthly home. Others have struggled with fear of the greater unseen, but You gave them strength and they found their way to Me in the end.

"But some here have called Our plan, Our promise, and the paradise We have prepared for them, lies. They have even taught their sad misconceptions to the innocent and have converted honest seekers to their hopeless beliefs. Hidden sorrow, poverty of spirit and bitterness consume them while they proclaim themselves needful of nothing. They spread their doctrines with self-appointed importance and do not see that they are the ones who have fallen prey to the real deception. You grant them their seasons of life here in this pond, that they may have time to seek and learn, but they live them in selfishness. The Wind calls them so that We may feed them with truth, but they do not listen. They know I am here, but they turn their backs and swim away."

As he spoke these words, a look of such deep sadness came upon the fisherman's face that the Old One felt a stab of sympathy. Although he didn't know why the man's sorrow should have anything to do with him, an uncomfortable feeling told him it did.

"I do not weary of coming to these waters, Father. But there is a certain one here whom I have long sought. My love for him has spanned many seasons and years. I have sensed his longing and have compassion

because of the fear that is mingled with his desire to know Me. His time is short, now. He has lived a long, brave life, but he has always ignored or avoided Me and has turned a deaf ear to My calls. He has even worked against Our purposes at times.

These things and more, You know, for he is Your creature. But this is my petition, Father – that You forgive and pardon him so that he may be freed from the chains of pride and mistrust that have bound him for so long. He does not realize that it was the very cries of his soul that brought Me here. For the first time, and perhaps the last, he is yearning for truth and for deliverance from his lonely existence. I believe that if he is given one more chance, the force of his desire will bring him to Me."

Below, the Old One floated motionlessly, giving no indication that he'd heard the words spoken above. His eyes were locked on the fisherman, and inside his heart a battle was raging. He was at war with himself – his calculating mind proposing clever evasive maneuvers and screaming out logical explanations to discredit the powerful, burning emotions within. No sound interrupted the silence around him. No other creatures moved. It seemed as though nothing and no one existed but the Old One and the fisherman.

Then, a familiar sound came from the forest. The Wind – rushing through the tops of the trees and swirling down upon the pond. Ripples raced across the surface and the old fish strained to see through them to the bridge. The Wind tousled the fisherman's hair and ruffled the shirt at his waist. He smiled with delight and lifted his arms upward in welcome. When he did so, a brilliant light poured down over him and he was transformed into a Being of such radiance that The Old One could scarcely look upon him.

The Wind blew wilder and harder. It whistled through the weathered planks of the old bridge and sent torrents of leaves down upon the pond. And then, the sounds became words. They were barely understandable at first, and perhaps not discernable to anyone listening less intently than The Old One. The voice was gentle, yet mighty. Stern, yet comforting. All powerful. All loving. And it came not only from above, but from *within* the waters. It was the voice of the Creator.

"Fisherman...My Son. Well do You know the depths of My mercy to call upon it on behalf of this old fish. Saving his own skin has always been his main concern. For that, he took the credit, and never looked higher. If he had, he would have seen You intercept the hooks

184

that were intended for him. They pierced and tore Your flesh instead of his, but he took no notice, for he'd already turned his back and swum away.

"He thanks Me for the beauty of his little earthly pond, yet he grants Me no capacity for further power or greater love beyond this small expression of Myself which he is able to feel with his senses. He has steadfastly rejected You, Whom I have sent so that he might know My plan. He believes that all cycles begin and end only in and around this place, and has therefore made his bed where he willed. As a result, he has lived a life void of true joy, love, and the comfort I could have given him.

He is the center of his own universe and boasts of no need for the hope of Our promise, nor will he trust that I have prepared a better home for him when his days here come to an end. He has refused Our counsel, Our companionship and Our help. He does not know Us. Oh, how harsh his self-inflicted struggles have been. And now, at his end, how deep is the pain of his loneliness as a result!

"Yes. All of these things I have seen. But because You, My beloved Son, have suffered long, cared for him unceasingly, and have asked it of Me, I shall remember them no longer. Our truth shall awaken his heart this very moment, if he allows, and he will be shown what it means to reach beyond himself. Within his soul there still exists the capacity for love, and though he thinks it impossible, an end can come to his loneliness through the realization of Who We are.

But I cannot influence his decision. The order of My creation forbids it. I can only release him from all that has gone before. He must choose to come to You."

The last words hit their mark deep within The Old One's heart — or was it is mind? The ferocious battle had abruptly ceased and he wasn't certain which was in control. His thoughts were no longer cold, calculating, fearful or suspicious. Feelings of warmth and anticipation pulsed through him instead, compelling him to swim closer to the bridge.

There was no doubt about the voice. No one but the Creator could know him so well. He bowed his head in awe and humility, for he knew now that the fisherman he'd scorned and avoided was the Creator's Own Son, Who had come to this lowly pond to watch over him and spare him all of his days.

The clarity and peace that the Old One felt were like nothing he had ever experienced before. But did he dare trust this new heart of his?

Was there truly a place where he need never fear hooks and lines again? A paradise where he would swim in warm, placid waters with an abundance of food and sunshine...where he would be reunited with his family and the old friends who had already gone ahead...where he would once again experience the joy and love he had lost?

Others had tried to describe it to him in times past. They'd insisted that the Wind sang to them of the beauty and peace that awaited them there. He had laughed at them and called them gullible. Now, he ached with shame. How could he have been so blind, narrow-minded and foolish as to misinterpret, scorn and reject such love for so long? He hadn't looked beyond his own pride and determination to be the master of his own fate.

What fate? What had he been clinging to, anyway? Life in this tiny pond? Loneliness and a slow death? And why, in the face of this truth, was a part of him still holding back like some miserable, helpless captive, locked behind the bars of a prison he had built around himself over the many years?

Had he waited too long? Was it too late? The Creator had granted his release, and the Wind sang of a new life, but was the great longing within him strong enough to overcome the other voice that demanded he return to his murky hollow and face the bitter end he deserved?

He knew that he was not worthy of the gifts that had just been freely offered to him. His shame would never have allowed him to ask for them, nor could he have earned them even if he were granted a dozen more lifetimes. He was unable to comprehend such unconditional forgiveness and mercy, but for reasons he could not fathom, the Creator's Son had made the plea to His Father on the Old One's behalf.

If Their love was that far beyond his realm of thinking, wasn't it possible that the place They spoke of was also unlike any that he, or anyone who struggled for life down here in the pond could imagine? If he followed his heart now, all of the things he'd worked for, valued, and taken pride in throughout his life would no longer matter. He would be leaving them all behind.

"Old One ... come to Me, and rest."

The countenance of the Creator's Son had returned to that of a man. He leaned over the railing, called out for the last time, and dropped the net into the pond. His eyes shone with hope as they scanned the shallows over the Old One's hiding place, and then they pierced the water and looked straight into his soul.

The Old One could not meet that holy gaze. He did not have the courage to lift his eyes, nor could he move any other part of his body. The Fisherman waited for many moments, and finally, when the waters did not stir, His head dropped in unconcealed sorrow. Slowly, he drew up the empty net, and after one long farewell look, he turned to leave.

The pounding of his heart jolted the Old One from his paralysis. He, too, turned away, and plunged downward toward the frigid depths of the pond, swimming faster and deeper until the darkness engulfed him. Then, commanding every bit of his remaining strength, he spun around and streaked back upward toward the bridge, and with a. mighty surge, he shot up out of the water higher than he had ever jumped in his life. For one spectacular second, a wreath of water droplets sparkled and flashed like jewels in a royal crown upon his head – and in the next, he fell at the feet of the Great Fisherman.

*G*olden rain spilled from the sky, and tears of joy fell from The Great Fisherman's face as He knelt upon the bridge. Legend has it that one of those holy tears found its way down into the pond, and from that day on, the waters became sweeter and more plentiful than ever before.

(In case you are wondering, the Old One's greatest adventure didn't end that day. Although he would have preferred to leave with the Creator's Son, it was decided that he should return to the pond for a few more seasons so that he could make amends, clear up some misconceptions, tell his tale, and share his newly acquired knowledge with the others, whom he asked to pass it on. This, they have faithfully done for countless generations – which is, of course, how I came to hear the story I have told you today.)

187

S.G.Rose

"I, the Lord, am near to the multitudes who stand in the Valley of Decision.
Turn to Me now, while there is still time.
Give Me your heart, for I am gracious and merciful,
slow to anger, and full of loving kindness.
Rejoice that you are Mine...for I will do great things."

The Book of Joel, Chapters 2 & 3

188

KINGDOM COME

• Words from the Father •

"**M**y Children, you are members of a holy family. Love one another. Cover differences with My love. They are of no consequence in our eternity. I am One with you and We cannot be divided. When you allow My kingdom to manifest within you on earth, no manmade wall will be able to stand against that love."

৯৬

"**F**ollow My Son's example, for you are related to Him. Christ came forth from My heart. In this He is unique. In Him all prophets before and to come are embodied. Accepting and partaking of His Divine nature as well as His humanity makes you His brothers and sisters. His shed blood flows through your veins."

In Christ, My character was revealed. This was the purpose for which He came to live amongst you in the flesh – so that henceforth, men and women would know that their God felt and understood human suffering. He came so that you would know, while you are yet in the flesh, that you, too, can overcome the world.

৯৬

"**C**hrist came to show you, by example, the highest calling and triumph of love. It was the *manner* in which He lived that carried the message He came to impart. For though countless words of wisdom have been offered by many great souls over the centuries, He alone lived a perfect life in thought, word and deed. He never forgot His true home, His birthright, nor His distinct commission while on earth. He was in the flesh, but not bound by it, for He saw beyond it – into His, My, and your eternal domain, of which this – your fleeting present existence – is but an infinitesimal part.

৯৬

189

"It has been said that 'there are many paths up the mountain,' and this is true. But however you arrive, My Son will be waiting for you at the top. He is the destination and the gateway. He cannot be mistaken for another, nor does He wear different faces. Mirrored in Him is My image. When you open your life to Him, others will see Him mirrored in you. Every comfort and truth you seek lies within Him."

∽

"Christ's sacrifice was His spotless life, surrendered for mankind. Man's sacrifice must be his pride. No one had the power to take My Son's life from Him. He willingly laid it down as a ransom to free you from darkness. He was sent as the Light to show you that you could be with Me as He is with Me. The weakness of the flesh called 'sin' is the roadblock to that perfect union. It constantly threatens to divide Father and children, to diminish the fullness of our relationship, and to rob you of your promised inheritance.

Through your acceptance of Christ's completion of His commission, the issue of sin is conquered. This absolution seems so simple that many either stumble over it or dismiss it. For you all, the first step is the bravest, for this access to forgiveness through one man's sacrificial act can only be accepted and activated by humble faith.

Throughout the ages, men and women have attempted to overcome the fatal weaknesses of their flesh by their own logic and power. But laws, punishments, penance, rituals, sacrifices and religions by the thousands have all failed to cleanse you. There was only one way to set you free: to become flesh and take your place."

∽

"For every individual, there comes a day of awakening. When you know truth, it will set you free. These are chaotic, perilous days for your souls. Do not be so wrapped up in the cares of this world, or in striving or worry, that you miss that day. For, when that time comes, it shall be as it was in the time of Passover, when those who heard and obeyed My warning were spared death by marking the door posts of their houses with the blood of a spotless lamb. They did not understand this symbolism, but they obeyed their God.

My Son left His seat in Heaven and came willingly to be the sacrificial lamb for all of you. When you believe this, your hearts will be marked with His blood, and you will be sealed and recognized for who you are, to Whom you belong, and in Whom you trust.

My heart grieves that any soul would not welcome, give thanks for and rejoice in this deliverance from evil. It is flesh that stubbornly rises up to rebel and resist. The wisdom of God seems foolish to man.

As long as men exalt their own philosophies over eternal truth; as long as they claim power with their own hands; as long as they seek to rule over and bring their brothers and sisters into submission, there will be the shedding of innocent blood. Christ's was shed for you so that you would no longer have to live as slaves to sin, but as free souls to whom I have given The Promised Land."

✦

"Listen to your innermost voice. I have promised that those who seek Me with all their hearts shall find Me. I have told you that I stand at the door of your life and knock, and that I will enter in and share Myself with those who open to Me. Do not look to others. Look to Me. Seek to hear Me. When you do this daily, I *will* guide your steps. Do not be led astray, confused or discouraged by the many different voices of men. Be patient, be prepared, and watch. In quietness and in confidence you shall discover your strength."

✦

"I am Spirit. I am not limited. Your souls live eternally in Me. They abide in the flesh that houses them on the earth for only a brief time. Let your existence be *My* concern as your Creator. If you cannot cause even one more hair to grow from your heads by thinking about it, what makes you think you can control your own destiny? Many have forgotten that they do not belong only to themselves, but also to their Creator and their Savior. Self, when it takes over the seat of God,

191

becomes anti-Christ – the soul's most dangerous enemy. Without exception, you will all one day come to the end of yourselves on the earthly plane. Listen to My words and heed them as a trusting child reveres the wisdom of a loving Father. Blessed are My little ones whose security and trust are in Me, alone."

❧

"I come to you veiled in clouds, yet those with keen hearts see me and run toward Me with great joy, while others stare and see nothing. I seek you all. I call you all. I shine upon you all. The veils are upon the eyes of the flesh, not the spirit. When a heart longs for Me, I lift the veil. Those who have turned away need only turn around again to find Me there. When you are weak, I am strong. When you see Me, you shall become like Me."

❧

"How, then, when My power is omnipotent to keep you, can fear, pain, or any tribulation alter your charted course or the destination of your soul? They cannot! In the moment you grasp this revelation, you shall be transformed. Your soul shall see its true path, and no man will have the power to dissuade or deceive you."

❧

"The day is coming when shades of gray shall disappear and all choices will become black or white. Good or evil. Darkness or light. Those with spiritual eyes to see and ears to hear can observe this division beginning now. The wide, easy path – the comfort zone where so many dwell – will narrow to a knife edge upon which no man will be able to stand. Many who have departed from truth and have walked willfully in paths of evil will fall to their knees in shame and repentance. Pain has darkened and scarred their minds, and in their sickness and blindness they have struck out against the innocent and the righteous. Their eyes will be opened to the lies that have held them captive, and they shall see the truth of their deeds. Sorrow will overwhelm them and open the door for repentance, forgiveness and healing. There is no sin so great that I shall not forgive it for the sake of My Son, who intercedes for you all."

∾⟨⟩

"**D**o not fear the things that are to come at the end of this age, for I will direct you at the appointed time. All that has been foretold shall come to pass, and there will be no question as to what the prophecies mean when they are fulfilled before your eyes.

While the world watches for colossal signs, know this: like a row of dominoes set strategically on end, all things in Heaven and Earth are moving into position. Because the pieces have been aligning over centuries, and because many have been placed without mankind's realization of their significance, the full picture cannot be seen or understood by men. Consider that it may not be a cataclysm, but just one small nudge that will set in motion an unstoppable chain of events.

I do not hide things from My children nor neglect to warn them. I have no favorites amongst you, nor do I dispense exclusive revelations to select individuals or groups. All of you will see the signs if you look for them. I have already sent many.

Your greatest challenge will be to continually sift and separate grains of truth from the chaff of misconceptions and deceptions. Falsehoods have always been taught, but these are now rampant and threaten to cause great confusion amongst you. As they have throughout the ages, they wear many fashionable disguises.

I am not the God of confusion. Your enemy, the evil one, is its author, and he masquerades as an angel of light. I have warned that wolves roam amongst you dressed as sheep. The hunting is easiest where the trusting, unsuspecting flock gathers, but I am faithful to expose and remove these pawns of the Deceiver in My time.

When you see these things come to pass, do not be discouraged. Instead, learn. You cannot fight in My army until you know the voice of your Captain. Heed and follow Me, alone."

∾⟨⟩

"Many souls are led astray when they do not challenge or question spiritual, social, political and moral trends. It is more convenient to accept the cup of water that is passed to them than to travel to the river; easier to listen to men than to seek My voice; more comfortable to stand with the popular majority than alone.

You live on the edge of a world where the unrelenting pressure of a rapidly-changing tide erodes virtue daily. Scores of weaker souls have been seduced away from higher ground, and have been led to a shifting shore. There, each wave washes away more sand from beneath their feet, and they sink deeper. If they stay, it will only be a matter of time before they are swept out to sea.

Climb to the rock, put down roots, and I will anchor you there, safely above the great sorrows to come. Though you may stand alone – *stand* – and you will witness the fulfillment of these words."

*

"There are powerful souls walking amongst you who refuse to compromise truth. Join their number. Before My Son was crucified, He prayed for those He loved. He asked not that I spare them from tribulation or take them out of the earth, but rather that I strengthen them so that they could endure what was to come. When you know Me, you will pray according to My will, as He did. He knew that the flesh is as the grass of the fields. It springs up, stands for a short time, fulfills its purpose, and then passes away. You are more than flesh."

*

"My beloved Children – do not fear suffering, for My strength is yours! My angels surround you, your souls have been fit with holy armor and the shield of faith shall prevail. Those who threaten to imprison, harm or kill your body cannot touch the soul that is hidden in Me. Your brothers and sisters who have suffered for the sake of freedom and truth understood this.

Every drop of righteous, innocent blood is more precious than rubies. I shall turn your tribulation to triumph, and your sorrows shall

194

become the jewels in the crowns I place upon your heads when you have overcome the world."

⌘

"Every soul who enters earth's experience is affected by many deaths to the flesh during the course of the human lifetime. Whenever one of these deaths is yielded to and appropriately interpreted, selfishness is further diminished and spiritual enlightenment grows in its place, resulting in less darkness and more light.

Within this expansion of awareness, there is room for a greater expression of the attributes of My nature. Even now, you can look back and understand this. Count your deaths to things your flesh held dear. Then count your rebirths as a stronger soul with a greater capacity for compassion, wisdom, understanding, and vision – the qualities born within the process of release and acceptance.

For now, you are pilgrims in a foreign, savage land. I am with you on the mountain top and in the valley of the shadow of death. My eyes are upon you in battle. Whatever your enemy, I will march before you, behind you, and on both sides.

Your victory shall be Mine – and Mine, yours. As a royal scarf is tied around the arm of a champion, so do I bestow My blessing upon My children as I send them forth.

Your life is eternal, and My hand rests always upon you. I have created you in My image and I am your Defender. I have sent you to love one another as I love you – to empower and heal one another as I empower and heal you. I am the Keeper of your souls, your Father and your God.

We are invincible."

⌘

S.G.Rose

FEAR NOT
♦ *An Illumination of Isaiah 43:1-5* ♦

"...I have created you.
Fear not, for I have redeemed you.
I have called you by your name and you are Mine.

"When you pass through the waters, I will be with you..."
For I AM the waters.

"And when you pass through the rivers, they shall not overflow you."
For I AM the rivers.

"And when you walk through the fire you shall not be burned;
neither shall the flame kindle upon you..."
For I AM the fire.

"Since you have been precious in My sight,
You have been honorable, and I have loved you..."
With a love deeper than any waters
through which you may have to pass.
With a passion more powerful than the mightiest current
of the broadest river.
With a desire hotter than any fire
through which you may have to walk.

Remember this, then, when the storms rage
or the flames surround you.
Look for Me there in your midst and know
that I AM within, above, beneath and all around you.
I have journeyed there with you, I shall lead you through,
and we shall walk out together.

FEAR NOT – *I am with you.*

♦

$\mathcal{S}$elah Gayle Rose was born in a small Western Washington town in 1948. She spent her childhood exploring the forests, mountains and waters of the majestic Pacific Northwest, where a love for nature, literature and the arts took root at a young age.

As the daughter of a Serbian mother and part Native American father, she feels a deep connection to the courage and spirituality of her ancestors.

"Whatever form my work takes, I am motivated by the desire to inspire and encourage others. Creativity is a Divine flow without end, and as its channels, we're designed to share what we've received. It's my assignment – my passion, purpose and calling."

A published multi-media artist and writer of 35 years, Gayle's writings and images have found their way around the world. *The Voice of the Spirit* was first published in 1999, and has been updated and expanded in this new edition.

A collection of Gayle's images and poems can be viewed in her online gallery at www.sgrose.com, where signed copies of this book may also be ordered.

Gayle and her husband Lance, live in the shadow of Washington State's Cascade Mountain range. They share four grown children and three grandchildren.